Room to Grow

Creating and Managing
the Self-Contained Special Education Class

Sylvia Gappa
Deirdre Glynn

Fearon Teacher Aids
a division of
PITMAN LEARNING, INC.
Belmont, California

The material on pages 142–143 is from "The Graded Word List: Quick Gauge of Reading Ability," in *Journal of Reading,* copyright January 1969. Reprinted with permission of the authors, Margaret LaPray and Ramon Ross, and the publisher, International Reading Association.

Editorial director: Roberta Suid
Editor: Peter Cross
Production editors: Patricia Clappison, Zanae Jelletich
Designer: Susan True
Photographer: Catherine Coates
Technical artist: Rosemarie Singer

ISBN-0-8224-5875-6
Library of Congress Catalog Card Number: 80-81682
Printed in the United States of America.
1 . 9 8 7 6 5 4 3 2 1

‖Contents

Introduction

We met in the fall of 1968—two eager, young teachers assigned to adjacent primary classrooms in a public school in the San Francisco Bay Area. One of us already had two years experience, the other was a novice. We both started that year sharing the feeling that we would correct the educational woes of the world and lead our students into the delights of learning, all in an orderly, graceful fashion.

Were we ever surprised! We had prepared well: a lot of reading-readiness work, a good perceptual-motor program, as well as putting together carefully assembled and rather clever reinforcement materials. But after a number of months, we found we had a total of four children who stubbornly refused to learn anything related to reading or writing, and nine others who, for no apparent reason, were far behind the children who seemed similarly mature and intelligent. Added together these two groups made up about one-fourth of our students.

Of more pressing concern, though, was that some of these children were driving us to distraction. One first grade boy in particular was a problem. He hit other children, swore at the noontime supervisor, and seemed unable to follow the school rules. We had to move him and his desk a safe distance from the others. Reports filtered in from other children's mothers that he was a mean, destructive brat. But we also knew that he executed the most beautiful paintings in the class, loved to hold

1

and stroke the class pet, and sometimes displayed an unusually mature sense of humor. He also seemed to be rather bright. His father told us that he was able to take apart and completely reassemble a full-sized bicycle!

This child was our introduction to learning disabilities. Now such disabilities are widely recognized as one of the principal reasons that seemingly capable children fail to learn, but such was not the case in 1968. Only gradually did we become aware that something unusual characterized the learning and behavior patterns of most of the problem children in our classes. The more we became aware of that something, the more it fascinated us. During that year and the next one, we spent more and more time talking with each other about these children. We brainstormed to find ways to teach them and help them manage their actions. We began to take classes and read everything we could find about learning disabilities. In our third year we struck a bargain with the other teachers—we would take increasing numbers of the learning disabled and behavior problem children into our rooms, as long as we could keep our classes small. They agreed to teach larger classes so that we could work with these special students.

Our common interests led us to further training and a brief stint as specialists. For six years now we have taught two self-contained special classes for the learning disabled in our district. (There are presently five.) We team teach one class of 24 students because the maximum per teacher in this type of program in California is 12 students. This group of 24 is the Special Class referred to in this book. Although the office still has 12 students listed in each of our homerooms, the staff, parents, administration, and social workers deal with us as if we had one group of 24 students.

We first began writing about our teaching work from a need to organize it for ourselves. We began to realize that a total program, all the parts of which are thoughtfully considered and reconsidered over and over again, is crucial to success with learning disabled children. Working with them is an intricate mixture of small-group and individualized remediation, image building, training in self-control and communication, and almost perpetual handling of conflicts. Many of the children need help in all these areas, and failure to help a child in one may prevent success in all the others. A teacher of the learning disabled needs to be aware of many things simultaneously, and have a wide range of sensitivities and behaviors always ready. At least, that's the goal. Truly understanding what it requires to teach in this way usually entails several years of doing it. Even so, we felt there must be an easier way to get at least a piece of that understanding.

Room to Grow thus became what we call a "textbook from experience." A textbook because it presents a management system and strategies which are applicable to many situations, and the rationale underlying them. But we recommend only those systems and strategies that are drawn from experience, the ones that are used with our program and the children we teach. It would have been impossible to write any other way. We want novice teachers, in particular, to know how children act in the context of a special program, and how our strategies relate to their problems. Although we describe actual situations, the names of the children and details of their cases have been changed to prevent the identification of any individual children.

We have found no substantial conflict between what we advocate (and our reasons for advocating it) and the general literature on the subject of learning disabilities. We have both earned advanced degrees in this field, and have read widely in it. We feel the overall program and specific practices described in this book can succeed with most learning disabled children.

We wrote *Room to Grow* thinking of both pre-service people (students of special education) and teachers who were already working with learning disabled children. The pre-service student can now find excellent texts describing remedial teaching in the basic areas. No book can replace experience, but *Room to Grow* can supplement these texts and give the pre-service student a feel for the total experience and the kinds of capabilities required of a special class teacher. And it is our hope that the book can alleviate some fears about working with the learning disabled child.

Teachers who are now working with such children will be interested in the more detailed suggestions in the book—plans for testing, record keeping, behavior management, and the like. We have learned a great deal from colleagues and from the plethora of magazine articles available; we are pleased to be able to make a contribution in return. We emphasize our particular use of a class meeting, and recommend it to both beginning and experienced teachers—we don't believe this practice is widely used with learning disabled children, and feel it is a key factor in our successes.

A special class program benefits the students *most* if it, and they, are accepted as part of their school. A school staff can, for example, help reduce the cruelty regular students often mete out to members of a special class, and often a special class teacher can share insights into the problems of beleaguered regular students.

Finally, we hope this book communicates the sense of the unique rewards to be found in this field. Paradoxically, working with children many perceive as difficult (and they often are), has given *us* real opportunities for growth. As we so often see it falter, and try to understand why, we have become aware of the extremely complex nature of learning. We have been inspired by the courage of our young charges, many of whose egos have been badly battered, and yet who need only a little encouragement to push back the feelings of failure and try again. We have learned there are no easy solutions in this area of education, or in any other—just a lot of hard work and continual reappraisal. But we have also seen over and over again how that work and reappraisal do indeed create room to grow.

Sylvia Gappa
Deirdre Glynn

1

‖ What They Need

Fifteen years ago the term *learning disability* was not a familiar one. This particular syndrome had not been mentioned in any of our undergraduate courses. Only after experiencing children who could neither learn in nor adjust to a regular school situation did we begin to investigate the possible causes of their disabilities.

After checking out a couple of graduate classes, picking the brains of several experts, and doing a lot of reading on our own, the term *learning disability* began to take on more meaning. Other terms soon joined the ranks: *dyslexia, educationally handicapped, minimal brain damage, word blindness,* and *perceptually handicapped.* The current California State Master Plan for Special Education uses the term *learning handicapped.* Studies by the Department of Health, Education, and Welfare usually use the term *minimal brain dysfunction syndrome.* All these labels refer to children with near-average to above-average intelligence who exhibit certain learning or behavioral problems. A learning disability does not indicate any impairment in intelligence itself.

We prefer to use the terms *learning disabled* and *learning disabilities,* as we feel they are kindest to the children, and most accurately indicate that a person has a specific difficulty or blockage in the ability to process information. This inability can lead to problems in handling one or more of the basic curriculum areas: reading, expressive and receptive language skills, handwriting, spelling, and mathematics. One must remain conscious, though, of the fact that the initial disability will probably be difficult to see at first because it easily becomes compounded with behavioral disorders of varying degrees. These disorders usually become intensified as the children battle to cope with a regular classroom situation.

‖ Two Children

The following case studies provide some insight into the personalities and difficulties of those children who aren't able to cope in regular classrooms, and have been referred to a Special Class program.

ALEX

It's always good to start with a success story, so let's begin with a boy we'll call Alex, age seven. Alex fairly represents many learning disabled children whose initial disability leads to broader social and behavioral difficulties.

Kindergarten was apparently relatively uneventful for Alex. A few comments in his records indicated that he had some fine-motor problems, that he had not met with much success in a beginning reading program, and that he occasionally had demonstrated some physical aggression toward his peers. But nothing else was noted.

By the end of kindergarten, Alex was categorized as "somewhat immature, but appears to have adequate potential" and passed on to the first grade where the trouble really started. Alex was unable to meet the rigorous demands of a formalized reading and writing program. He began to resist the only way he knew how—by refusing to do the work. Several times he told the teacher that he wasn't even going to attempt the task at hand, and that there was no way she could make him want to try.

When Alex found he couldn't gain attention from his peers by participating successfully in group activities, he took the usual alternative routes to getting attention—loud and unruly behavior. As a result, Alex spent more and more time sitting in the hall, sitting in the principal's office, and sitting in his room when he was sent home from school. Of course none of this had any educational value, so he fell further behind in his school work.

Alex came to our Special Class at the beginning of second grade, his third year in school. Chronologically, he was a second grader. Academically, he was functioning at a beginning first grade level in all areas except expressive language, which was age appropriate if not higher. Socially, Alex usually isolated himself, and alienated other children with his aggressive behavior.

Formal testing conducted by the case psychologist indicated strengths in the following areas: average-to-above average intelligence, good visual memory, well-developed abstract reasoning, and advanced oral language skills. The psychologist reported major deficits in auditory discrimination, auditory memory, visual motor skills, attendance to tasks, and social interaction.

We began to remediate Alex's problems with the following techniques, all of which will be more fully described in later chapters:

- A basic sight approach was used in reading since Alex's strength lay in visual memory. We taught him the vocabulary in three preprimers from an old state reading series without using the books. (Alex objected strenuously to anything vaguely resembling "baby" materials.) We then started to have him use a hardcover primer which both satisfied his ego and corresponded to his true reading level.

- So as to learn the sound-symbol relationships for the letters of the alphabet, sound blending, and all the upper and lowercase manuscript forms, Alex participated in the Slingerland multisensory method. (Additional discussion of Slingerland is found on page 59.) This approach was effective in helping Alex overcome visual-motor problems, and by midyear the program brought noticeable improvement in his handwriting. Alex was able to learn most of the sound-symbol relationships, but continued to have discrimination problems, particularly between *b* and *p*, and *b* and *d*, and the short *e* and *i*. We encouraged him to use his newly acquired sound-blending skills during reading periods.

- By using a manipulative approach to mathematics, math turned out to be an area of strength for Alex. His lack of growth in the past seemed a result of his refusal to complete tasks. He rapidly completed a first grade program, and by midyear Alex moved into a second grade program.

- A behavior management system based on reinforcement for positive behaviors helped Alex improve his peer interactions and attendance to tasks. Alex was required to complete all individual work in an office using a red flag system. (For more on the office system see pages 45–47.) This arrangement meant that Alex had to ask for teacher assistance in an appropriate way. His positive behaviors were rewarded by points (pages 74–77), and his negative ones were generally ignored. We also utilized "time-outs" (ten-minute isolation periods) whenever Alex would yell and when his interruptions prevented other members of the class from working.

- We also employed the point system to reinforce positive peer relationships. This system, along with class discussions and individual conferences on how to make friends and influence people, began to help Alex recognize the advantages of belonging to a group. By the end of the year, we saw a significant decrease in the annoying mannerisms and physical aggression that isolated him from other children. Alex wasn't the most popular child on the block yet, but he wasn't an outcast either.

By the end of his first year in the Special Class, Alex was standing on his own two feet—rather shakily, but standing. He was asking us for help in order to complete a task rather than allowing vague frustrations to disturb him. Alex was no longer blaming other children for disrupting his work, and he was completing most tasks independently. He was also learning to read. Alex returned for a second year to firm up his new-found skills and to continue improvement in his attitude and behavior.

Alex's Graduation

By the midpoint of his second year, we decided that Alex was ready to try a regular third grade class. Fortunately, a third grade teacher in our own school had expressed empathy for learning disabled children, and so we enrolled Alex in her class. The time that Alex spent there was gradually increased until by year's end he was going full time. To be sure, Alex had a few relapses, but he—and the teacher—were able to handle them. In the fall, Alex returned to his home school for fourth grade.

Later that year, we received a note from the speech therapist who had worked extensively with the "old" Alex. She wrote, "Thank you for turning the frog into a prince." That vote of appreciation made our day for many days, and we still have the note.

GEORGE

We include the story of George to illustrate some of the severe problems a Special Class teacher may encounter. This case may seem to be an extreme one, but in all likelihood anyone who teaches this kind of program for more than one year may well work with a child with comparable problems.

George was eleven when we took over the Special Class. His record of difficulties began at age five. He was asked to leave the regular kindergarten class after only a few weeks of attendance. The school recommended that he be removed from the public school setting because of his extremely immature behavior. The immature behavior included the child's inability or refusal to sit in a chair for more than a few seconds at a time, refusing to hang up his coat, drooling at snacktime, an inability to tie his shoes, refusing to follow directions—the list of refusals goes on.

Because George had been previously diagnosed as borderline cerebral palsied, he was enrolled in a county-supported kindergarten program for children with severe gross- and fine-motor problems. The following fall George was placed in the Special Class, and he was still there three years later when we first met him.

He demonstrated average intelligence, and it was clear that he could gain information through listening if he would only sit still long enough to do so! George had numerous deficits: severe motor problems, both gross- and fine-motor; he was unable to express himself coherently; his math and writing skills were at a beginning first grade level; reading skills were at a beginning second grade level; hyperkinesis (which was being treated with Ritalin); and aggressive behavior patterns that prevented him from making any advances academically and alienated his peers.

George got frustrated easily and his anxiety level was high. The slightest demand made upon him—a paper to do, a peer confrontation, or a warning by the yard supervisor to stop bouncing a ball off another child's head—resulted in a screaming tirade of obscenities accompanied by physical violence against himself and others. The tremendous energy he dissipated during these outbursts quickly reduced him to infantile behavior, often ending in his taking a fetal position on the floor. In that state, he would often sob and suck his fingers.

We immediately initiated behavior modification with the specific purpose of increasing attending behaviors. But that was not enough, and we could not find a way to give George the exclusive attention he so angrily demanded. It took a very disturbing incident to shake us into realizing that our program alone was not sufficient.

George had been sent on a "time-out" for disturbing the group during physical education in the cafeteria. Although he was angry, he seemingly had not lost control in the usual way. But suddenly his body became rigid. George quickly turned and put his fist through a plate glass window, shattering it. The whole chain of events seemed to have moved in slow motion: the glass flying, sparkling and tinkling to the floor, and the bright red drops of blood dripping down his pants, splattering on the concrete. We both stood there, shocked, for what seemed a long time; in fact, only a few seconds had passed. We headed full speed for the nurse's office while one of our aides, with her usual calm, hurried the rest of the children back to the classroom.

George's physical injuries healed quickly. However, his emotional wounds continued to fester. At our insistence, counseling was initiated at a local mental health clinic. George received a physical and neurological examination that resulted in the elimination of the daily dosages of Ritalin. He was entering his prepuberty growth stage and it was felt that the medication was no longer effective. All the experts agreed that George was an extremely disturbed youngster.

George's Transition

As the last quarter of our year with him approached, we were forced to make some hard decisions. George had demonstrated little academic growth. His attention span was still no more than a few minutes, and even the most minor environmental stimulus distracted him. Most of his energy was directed into activities, primarily wandering about the room, that would allow him to avoid the task at hand.

We pursued placement for George in a county class for severely emotionally disturbed children. He qualified, but they didn't have a space for him. Finally, through the efforts of a mental health clinic counselor, he was admitted to a private educational facility for disturbed children. He still attends such a school, and at the time of this writing George has just turned fifteen. We are quite concerned because his chances of leading a normal adult life seem slim at this point.

|| Assessment: The First Step

The stories of Alex and George show more than just the range of problems with which a Special Class teacher may have to cope. They also point up the need for early and exact assessment of the child's abilities and disabilities, and for evaluation of the degree to which behavioral problems have developed in the wake of school failure. Alex, as we noted, came to us from second grade, but he also came to us after we had been working together with the Special Class for several years. We were able to quickly and accurately pinpoint his deficits and teach to his strengths. The successes he began to experience made it easier for him to normalize his behavior. George, however, was a member of the first Special Class we taught as a team, and had made little progress during the previous four years. In the earliest years of his difficulties, not only was there less awareness of learning disabilities among teachers, but there were also fewer resources available for handling such children. In this sense George is a victim of history. Had George come along six or seven years later, perhaps his story might have been different. He would not only have come to us much younger, but we would have been able to plan his work on the basis of a more sophisticated system of assessment than was available when he was first assigned to a special program.

When a child is referred to us, and then enters our class, we want to get to know that child thoroughly as soon as we can. It is not enough to simply leaf through his file or discuss his history with former teachers. We always supplement the school system's and previous teachers' assessments with our own, and only when we have completed the entire pattern do we feel we have a solid foundation for proceeding with the child's program.

TESTING THE NEW STUDENT

We first begin to find out about a new child when we review the results of the formal testing as completed by the case psychologist. These results are presented at the Educational Assessment Service (EAS) meeting at the district level. Usually, the psychologist has already administered the Weschler Intelligence Scale for Children (WISC), the Wide Range Achievement Test (WRAT), the Bender Gestalt Test, and the Peabody Picture Vocabulary and the Draw-a-Person tests. The psychologist's report identifies the child's strengths and weaknesses, but only as indicated by those tests. Usually the psychologist has not spent much time with the child.

At the same meeting, as most people now know, an Individual Educational Plan (IEP) is developed, which states the general educational goals and objectives for the child. These must be agreed upon by all members of the committee. We have found, however, that usually neither the standardized tests nor the meeting yields clear and workable objectives. At this point, we usually ask if it is acceptable for us to do further work with the child, and resubmit specific objectives to the committee. We then accept the child and, in the first few days of school, administer our own battery of tests.

We recommend using tests and methods that aid most directly in choosing specific teaching techniques to remedy weaknesses in reading, math, language, and perceptual-motor skills. Some of the tests are commercial. Others were developed by different sources and picked up at various workshops. Several of them were reworked to meet our own needs. The whole battery of tests is not usually administered to each child. Rather, we fill in the gaps left by previous testing so as to determine as closely as possible the child's current functioning level.

Testing is completed during the first three to four days of the new fall term, and the new students are divided into small groups of five to eight students. Only one such group comes to school on each of these first few days. Using the group system, the four of us (two teachers and two aides) can test each child individually and begin to get acquainted on a personal level. To prevent testing fatigue, the testing day is broken up with activity periods. (Children often simply get weary of the test pressures and begin to say anything to satisfy the examiner.) For example, a reading test may be administered, followed by an independent visual-motor test. Then an oral counting test and writing numbers test may be administered, followed by a bathroom break and a short recess.

While the children are being tested, their other behaviors should be observed, such as hand preference, pencil grip, level of eye contact, ability to respond to questions appropriately, anxiety level, and so on. We jot down notes on these behaviors right in the test margins so they can be incorporated later into an on-going anecdotal record (see pages 23–27).

To maintain organization and promote clarity, we developed a couple of basic guidelines for standardizing our testing procedures. Our tests are designed for use first in the fall, and then are rechecked in the spring. To reduce confusion, we recommend that *everyone* use the same color ink to record testing answers and results (for example, blue for fall and green for spring). We are also rigorous about recording the students' responses consistently. It's a simple system, involving only one or two types of markings to indicate mastery or correct responses. Our definition of mastery is the ability to give a correct response without *any* clues from the examiner. In many cases, mastery is indicated with a plus (+) sign. Other times, we circle the correct responses. The method of recording mastery should always be indicated in the directions at the top of each test. In this way, the information can be easily exchanged and interpreted by others in the team working with the child.

Standard Heading Format for Assessments

Student's Name _____
Age _____
Examiner _____
Fall Date _____
Spring Date _____

Title of Test

Directions: _____
_____

Mastery: _____

A standard heading format organizes important information in a consistent way to facilitate filing and access.

TESTING READING LEVEL

To provide information on the child's current functioning reading level, we give a combination of letter and word recognition tests and a phonics evaluation. Each of the following tests can be modified for use in all classes. Included below is an explanation of each test, how to use it, and, in most cases, the actual test itself. The tests are reproduced in the appendix (see pages 138–152).

Decoding Skills Test

This test covers upper and lowercase letter recognition, sound-symbol relationships for all consonants and short vowels, one-syllable short vowel words in both patterned and mixed vowel format, rudimentary two- and three-letter blends, and more advanced vowel patterns. This simple test is invaluable as a quick determiner of exactly where the child stands relative to basic phonetic word attack skills. Does the child need to learn letter names? Does the child know a few consonant sounds but no vowel sounds? Is the child confused about *b* and *d*? Does the child quickly read the patterned short vowel words but stumble through the mixed vowels? This test also gives us a clue as to whether the child is using an auditory or visual approach to reading. Children using the auditory approach will often laboriously "sound out" each word when reading, while children using the visual approach read words fairly rapidly.

Color Word Recognition Test

This test checks a child's ability to recognize the basic colors and his ability to read the basic color words. Since color words are often used in both oral and written directions, it is important that the child be able to identify these words and match them to their respective colors. If the child has difficulty with this test, design his or her reading program to include color word recognition practice.

Basic Sight Words Test

This test is based on the well-known Dolch lists. The words are classified by levels. Level I is equivalent to first grade words, Level II to second grade words, and Level III to third grade words. All the words are put on flashcards (sentence strips cut into six-inch lengths). The child is shown a flashcard. If a child reads the word correctly, a plus (+) sign is recorded in the appropriate box to indicate mastery. Incorrect responses are written in as given by the child for later error analysis. (We use the abbreviation *D.K.* to indicate a response of *Don't Know*.) The results of these tests are used as the basis for Word Study, a daily reading activity. When a flashcard is made for a child's

Word Study, a check is entered in the flashcard column. (For Word Study details, see Chapter 3.)

We have provided a sample of the format for the Level I test. Level II words, Level III words, and the advanced basic sight words, listed in the appendix (pages 135–137), are made into tests following the same format.

San Diego Quick Assessment Test

This test is an easy-to-administer and easy-to-correct word recognition test that correlates closely with basal word recognition tests like those provided by Ginn and Harper & Row. The difference is that the San Diego Quick Assessment, developed by Margaret La Pray and Ramon Ross, is used to obtain a preliminary estimate of a child's reading level for grouping purposes and to aid in selecting reading materials.

We have established a simple administering procedure. We type each graded word list on a separate 3 × 5 index card. Then the student reads the preprimer list of words aloud. We have the student continue to read from increasingly difficult lists until three words are missed on one list. We circle all correct responses on the examiner's copy and note all incorrect responses for future error analysis. The level at which the student misses no more than one word is the independent reading level. Two errors indicate the instructional reading level. Three or more errors on a particular level indicates what materials are likely to be too difficult. The examiner's copy given at the end of the chapter contains word lists from preprimer through tenth grade level.

Reading Series Graded Word Recognition Test

Most basal reading series provide their own word recognition test. Since most of the teachers in our district are presently using the Ginn reading series, we routinely give Ginn's test along with the San Diego Quick Assessment. The two tests check each other, and the Ginn test tells us where to find an oral reading sample for use as a further check on the child's reading level. As with the other tests, we keep comprehensive notes on the child's responses for later analysis.

On occasion, we also have utilized the following commercial tests:

Spache, George C., *Diagnostic Reading Scales*. Monterey, California: CTB/McGraw-Hill. 1963. (Del Monte Research Park, Monterey, CA 93940)

Wepman, Joseph M., *Auditory Discrimination Test*. Chicago: Language Research Association. 1973. (175 E. Delaware Place, Chicago, IL, 60611)

Woodcock, Richard W., *Woodcock Reading Mastery Tests*. Circle Pines, Minnesota: American Guidance Service. 1974. (Publisher's Building, Circle Pines, MN, 55014)

TESTING LANGUAGE SKILLS

During the testing we evaluate the child's knowledge of basic language concepts, his or her expressive language level, knowledge of the alphabet (both oral and written), handwriting skills, understanding of temporal concepts, and general self-knowledge. This information helps us plan language arts activities that correspond to the child's current functioning level. At this time, we also become aware of those children who may have deficits beyond the scope of our daily program and who, therefore, should be referred for additional speech and language therapy.

Temporal Concepts Test

This test evaluates understanding of such time concepts as before, after, days, weeks, and so on. A simpler version of the test that follows asks students to provide ages, birthdays, addresses, telephone numbers, mothers' and/or fathers' names, days of the week, months, seasons, and clock times. Deficits this test reveals can often provide a Special Class teacher with plenty to work on for the entire year!

Alphabetical Order Test

Have the child recite the alphabet without models and record omissions and confusions. Then have the child write both upper and lowercase forms without models. If the child cannot write the alphabet in order, dictate the letters at random. Keep notes on handedness, pencil grip, letter formation, spacing, and the format used on the paper.

Expressive Language Observation Test

In this informal test, we record the child's responses to an age-approximate picture, and have the child tell us about the scene presented. We write or tape-record *exactly* what the child says about the picture. Sometimes it's necessary to use prompting questions such as "Is there more to the story?" or "What will happen next?" to get enough material. We indicate these prompting questions with a question mark as a reminder that the child needed help in expressing ideas. If necessary, we show more than one picture to get a more complete sample of oral language patterns.

It's possible to gather a great deal of information from an informal language sampling. As the child responds to the picture, the following characteristics should be observed:

- **Articulation.** Is the child having difficulty with certain speech sounds that would necessitate a referral to the speech therapist?
- **Pitch.** Is the voice abnormally high, low, inaudible, hoarse, or broken? Should there be a referral to the speech and language therapist for a further check?
- **Fluency and Organization.** Does the child express ideas in coherent order, or does the child continually search for the right word, lose the train of thought, or jump from one idea to another?
- **Vocabulary and Syntax.** Are the child's vocabulary and syntax culturally and age appropriate? Does the child speak another language at home? Does the child use phrases, single words, or complete sentences when expressing ideas?
- **Appropriate Content.** Are the child's responses appropriate to the picture stimuli? Is the child able to expand ideas with creative imagination, or does the child give an obvious description of the picture?

Boehm Test of Basic Concepts

This 1971 commercial test is available from the Psychological Corporation, 304 E. 45th Street, New York, N.Y. 10017. The basic concepts tested (temporal, spatial, quantitative) are closely related to a child's ability to follow oral and written directions. (Never take for granted that a child understands what such words as on, over, below, and between mean!) The test is easy to administer and score. We give it in the fall and then work on teaching the concepts missed throughout the year.

TESTING MATH SKILLS

We give a series of math assessments to determine the child's current functioning level. This often presents an opportunity for the child to shine a little. Many learning disabled children are able to test well in math skills and to stay at or above grade level, providing the materials they are given are simply and clearly organized, and contain few written directions.

Oral Counting Test

The examiner's copy of this test contains typed numbers from zero to 200. First ask the child to start with zero and count by ones as far as he or she can. To score the test, cross out each number skipped or mispronounced and circle the last number the child says. After testing the child on counting by ones, check to see if he or she can count by twos, fives, and tens. Using a different color for each counting sequence, circle the last number the child says and indicate how far the child counted in the appropriate space at the bottom of the page.

Writing Numbers Inventory

This is simply a sheet of ditto paper with solid lines drawn ¾ of an inch apart. Ask the child to take the paper and, beginning with zero, write numerals as far as he or she can. We observe the child's ability to organize the task. Is the child able to progress across the line from left to right? Is a space left between each numeral? For young children (kindergarten and first grade) or older children who demonstrate an inability to organize at this level, we provide one-inch grid paper and direct them to write one numeral in each box. This test quickly reveals reversals, and the child's ability to understand a task involving a series of symbols which are to be presented in an orderly and consistent way.

Reading Numbers Test

This test tells us if a child can read up to one hundred. We also note if the student makes errors in transposition, such as reading *14* as *41* or *69* as *96*. The format on page 146 is the examiner's copy. To make the student copy, use a full 8½ × 11 sheet of paper and reproduce in large black print the grid of numbers shown.

Math Assessment Test

This test assesses basic computational skills in addition, subtraction, multiplication, and division. The "total possible" column on the record sheet indicates how many problems to develop for each category. The student copy should be mimeographed using primary typewriter numbers. Leave ample working space for computation. The space at the bottom of the examiner's record sheet marked "observations" is first marked "facts" or "manipulative." If the child is still at the manipulative stage, the objects manipulated—blocks, number lines, fingers, and so on, are noted.

TESTING PERCEPTUAL AND MOTOR SKILLS

Although one can glean a lot of information about children's perceptual-motor development by having them read and write letters and numbers, commercial tests can occasionally be used to fill in the details of an individual child's capabilities and development. We have successfully used the following two:

Beery, K. and Buktenica, N., *Developmental Test of Visual-Motor Integration.* Chicago: Follett Publishing, 1967.

Colarusso, P. and Hammill, D., *Motor-Free Visual Perception Test.* Novato, California: Academic Therapy Publications, 1972.

In most cases, however, we administered a simple physical skills test that provides sufficient information on gross-motor and lateralization skills and a test on identifying body parts.

Physical Skills Test

This test is a welcome break for most children during a heavy day of testing. It includes explanations for the examiner of what to look for and how to administer each section. Observations go on the record sheet that follows the test explanation sheet.

Parts of the Body Test

This test shows how well a child can correctly identify and locate parts of his or her own body. We focus on these parts when testing: hair, hands, feet, mouth, ear, nose, back, stomach, knees, teeth, heels, forehead, neck, cheek, chin, thumbs, nails, lips, shoulders, eyelashes, elbows, wrists, eyebrows, nostrils, calf, eyelids, ankles, hips, nape of the neck, cheekbones, forearm, temple, and palm. We use a format similar to the one used for the Color Word Recognition Test (see page 152). Later, through our physical education classes, we help the child develop a knowledge of the body parts identified incorrectly in this test.

INFORMAL OBSERVATION

We supplement our diagnostic testing with informal observations to create a more complete picture of the child. However, "informal" does not mean general. We look for behavior, competencies, and deficits of specific types. We begin these observations the day the child walks through the door and continue them throughout the year. They are recorded in an anecdotal record that is maintained on each child.

Classroom Interaction

How does the child approach other children? If Billy needs to borrow an eraser, does he grab it or ask for it? Does Mary stand off to the side and watch the other children, or does she go up

Anecdotal Record Sheet

Observations on Sam Smith	C = Classroom Observations
Year 1977–78	P = Parent Contacts
Gappa and Glynn	D = Support Services Contacts (District Office, etc.)

Date	
C 9/10/77	1st day in class—yelled out in loud voice—"I go," "You tell me," when asked to respond to test questions. Unable to complete testing. Did not follow oral direction—"Please get your coat." Had to be led to coat rack.
C 9/17/77	Responds to strong visual clues—i.e., couldn't make "a" in name properly—said "show me." Showed him, talking through steps. Able to make thereon. Beginning to follow simple routines—gets coat, lines up for recess, comes to class meeting circle.
P 9/28/77	Conference with mother. Stated she was eager to co-operate in any way. Stated there is a great deal of jealousy between Sam and younger brother (age 5). Sam doesn't really play with him, only teases. Mother said family would continue private language therapy and outside counseling. Signed permission slips for exchange of information between school and outside agencies.
C 10/5/77	Left chair in class meeting 3 times. Unable to state responsibility first 2 times when asked to. 3rd time said, "listening position." Remained in chair for rest of meeting.
D 10/10/77	Observed ½ hour by program psychologist. Will meet and discuss next Tuesday.

Anecdotal records noting classroom behavior, parent contacts, and district office observations help to verify the child's social-emotional growth.

and ask someone to play? In class meetings, does Joe look at other people when they are speaking, or does he fiddle with his belt?

Independent Work Habits

Is the child able to sit at a desk and complete an assignment at or below his or her functioning level without adult supervision? As we test the children at the beginning of the year, each has an opportunity to work in an independent folder containing four or five very simple tasks. These are dot-to-dot worksheets, coloring projects, alphabet fill-ins, visual comparison of basic shapes and the like, all of which are selected to be relatively easy for that child. We tell the child to not bother with those worksheets that are too difficult. This helps to keep frustration with the task itself reduced to a minimum. Of primary interest here is the child's ability (or inability) to work on his or her own. This is the time to collect data on problems such as distractability, inattentiveness, and avoidance behavior. If, for example, Johnny gets up from his desk to get paste and on his way touches Jane, sharpens his pencil, jams the keys on the typewriter as he passes it, and when he does get back to his seat, he looks up to count all the light fixtures and rearranges his crayons in several different configurations, we know that he's likely to avoid other tasks in a similar fashion. This child is going to require a lot of minute-by-minute direction.

Perceptual Difficulties

We extend the usage of certain tests to include a diagnostic appraisal of perceptual problems. The following are some examples. If, while being administered the Decoding Skills Test, Tony hesitates and calls a b a d, or vice versa, this is a strong indication of possible reversal or visual memory problems. While being administered the Alphabetical Order Test, Sandy writes a capital D rather than a lowercase d. Did she do so because she does not know how to make a small d, or did she use that means of writing to hide the fact that she can't remember which way the d goes? In the Physical Skills Test we also look for signals of gross-motor difficulties and left-right confusion.

When the child kicks a ball (assuming he or she can), is it with the right or left foot, or right one time and left another? These brief examples suggest something of how careful observation can add to the usefulness of many of the tests.

Self-image and Autonomy

Can Ralph get to the bathroom without adult supervision and still resist the compulsion to pull the fire alarm? Can he sit right next to someone in the cafeteria without poking his neighbor's cupcake—or his neighbor? Can he say hello to the principal, or does he creep like a shadow down the hall? Does he pick up his feet while walking to the library, or does he shuffle along as though he's uncomfortable with his body?

All of these assessments begin to build a composite image of a learning disabled child. But how do these assessments apply to real children in real situations?

A NOTE ON RECORD KEEPING AND TEST FORMS

It is obvious that by the time all this testing is complete, there is a considerable accumulation of papers for each student. We include here a brief description of our overall record keeping system, since it begins with a child's admission to the class and the initial assessments.

All the initial tests are filed. Later, we file examples of the child's work in the same folder, dating each sample. The examples are selected to show the child's progress and are attached (at least early on) to the appropriate test. For example, should the test show that a child could not write the alphabet from memory, we may also include a worksheet or a second trial of the test, confirming this inability. Later, a fully correct paper is included. We are absolutely sure to date each sample.

In addition to the tests-and-followup folder, we maintain another folder that contains records on academic skills and social/emotional growth. We use a sheet for each academic area to record information about the child's work in that area from previous school records as well as our testing results. Additional information is added as we continue to record tasks attempted, results, further tests, and the like. We also include in this folder our running observational record on the child. We consider it absolutely necessary to record only actual events and facts, and to avoid drawing any inferences from a child's actions or making any judgments. For instance, we might record "Sam had Tom's ball in his lunchpail. Tom said he did not give it to him." But we would never record "Sam stole Tom's ball today." We note significant social interactions with other children or teachers, episodes of note during recess or lunch periods, contacts with parents and support service people, and the like. Having this factual base available is invaluable when it comes to reassessing the child's program; answering questions from parents; or getting help from the administration, the district's psychologist, or other specialists.

When a child transfers back to a regular class or moves out of our district, all the reading and testing records and other data are combined into one file. They are labeled "Special Class" and inserted into the child's cumulative record in the school or district office.

In the appendix, on pages 138–152, are the assessment instruments we use that are in the public domain. It should be noted that these are the examiner's sheets. The actual tests for the children are in a range of forms as described on pages 14–23.

|| Using the Assessments: Walter's Program

Walter was tested extensively by a school psychologist prior to his arrival in the Special Class. He also had been seen by a number of professionals at the child study unit of a local medical facility. The consensus was that Walter's intelligence was in the average range and that his major strengths lay in receptive language and auditory memory. He had the most difficulty with gross- and fine-motor tasks, expressive language, and math concepts. Walter had completed second grade but he was functioning at a beginning first grade level in reading, math, and language arts. He was also beginning to experience social problems with his peers, and was feeling badly about his lack of success in school.

However, the testing didn't tell us exactly what Walter knew. The following is a brief summary of the tests we administered, how Walter performed, and how we planned his program using the information we gleaned.

READING

On the Decoding Skills Test, Walter identified twenty-four out of the of the twenty-six letters of the alphabet. He knew all the consonant sounds, but was unable to give short vowel sounds for *e* and *i*. He had more success with patterned phonetic words. On the San Diego Quick Assessment Test and a basal word recognition test, he scored at the primer level for instruction. In both cases, we observed that Walter relied on visual memory and attempted phonics only as a last resort. He knew all the color words and about one-third of the Level I Basic Sight Words.

The psychologist's testing indicated strong auditory memory, and Walter had been in a totally phonetic reading program for two years. However, he had made minimal progress. When we tested him, he seemed more comfortable using a visual approach. We put him in a primarily visual basal reader at a preprimer level and added auditory word-memory activities. Using the words missed on the Basic Sight Words Test, we emphasized efforts to build his sight vocabulary. He began to improve in reading.

LANGUAGE ARTS

On the Temporal Concepts Test, Walter performed well in all areas except months, seasons, and telling time. He missed only one item on the Boehm Test of Basic Concepts and was able to recite the alphabet in correct order. Writing the alphabet was another story. Walter mixed upper and lowercase manuscript forms, omitted several letters completely, and exhibited poor line placement and organization. Pencil grip was tense and awkward. His expressive language was hesitant and poorly organized. However, if a listener was willing to wait, Walter was able to get his ideas across.

We put Walter into a Slingerland multisensory program to help him learn correct letter formation. Kinesthetic tracing of the letters was used extensively. He began to learn how to type. (Neat penmanship will probably never be Walter's forte.) At the same time, he was learning both the sound-symbol relationship for all the letters and how to write a simple phonetic sentence with one-syllable short vowel words. Months, seasons, and expressive language skills were also practiced during language group and class meetings. Fortunately, Walter loved to share with his classmates and we all learned a lesson in patience as Walter slowly learned to express himself.

MATH

Walter knew only a couple of addition and subtraction facts under 10. He was unable to organize his numbers on the Writing Numbers Test, and he could only write to 21 when using a box grid. But he was able to count orally by ones to 129 and by fives to 100. He was able to read all the numbers except 21, which he called 12.

Obviously, Walter needed to learn some very basic computational skills. Beginning with addition (using blocks), he practiced daily with sums under ten. When he demonstrated that he understood the plus symbol, subtraction was introduced. Eventually the two were mixed. He progressed to facts to 18 and learned how to use a number line. He also learned how to tell time to the hour and half hour. Walter continued to use a grid when writing numerals in sequence. Math was hardly a joyful activity for Walter, but he was beginning to acquire basic math survival skills.

MOTOR ACTIVITY

Walter performed quite well on the Parts of the Body Test, only missing a few obscure items such as the nape and forearm. On the Physical Skills Test, however, he demonstrated difficulties with balance, running, jumping, skipping, and hopping. Walter was right-handed, left-footed, and right-eyed.

Participating in our low-key physical education program was ideal for a child with Walter's problems. Since there is no emphasis placed on competitive games, he didn't feel like the team reject. (Kids like Walter always get picked last.) Instead, he was able to work on basic body movements—running, skipping, hopping, and so on. We introduced him to yoga, which made him more sensitive to his body and its position in space. Granted, Walter may never be a major league ball player, but at least he will be able to move through space with some grace.

Based on the assessment of Walter's abilities, the educational program designed for him addressed his particular problems, provided specific learning experiences with his abilities in mind, and set the foundation for his success in the Special Class.

|| When the Child Arrives

Testing, objective assessment, and careful observation are all important components in teaching the learning disabled. But it is equally important to provide the child a measure of security, and help him or her assess *us,* with an accent on the positive. Always be aware that you are dealing with very special young people who find themselves in what they may perceive as a threatening situation. They usually have been uprooted from their home school, have to ride on a bus labeled "MR" by unknowing kids in their neighborhood, and find themselves in a class that does not look or operate like most regular classes. Often their arrival in the Special Class has been precipitated by very unhappy school experiences. Consequently, we spend a good deal of time orienting the children to the Special Class and developing in them a sense of acceptance.

ALLAYING FEARS

When testing the children during their first days in the class, they often give physical and verbal clues as to how they are feeling. Anxieties come up frequently. For example, a child may tremble, stutter, have difficulty making eye contact, and mumble answers to questions. In some cases, a student may come right out and ask, "Why am I here anyway?" This is a good time to be completely honest. We explain to the child that he or she is having trouble learning to read, write, or whatever the academic problem may be, and that we are there to help.

The child's main problem may not be academic in nature, but an emotional or social one. We might say, "You got into a lot of fights at your old school, and we're here to help you learn better ways to make friends." Actually, these first reactions to the Special Class are often based on a deep-seated fear which the learning disabled child finds difficult to verbalize—"Am I mentally retarded?" We bring this question up at initial class meetings and continue to deal with it as the need arises. We respond honestly, "No, you are not mentally retarded. You can learn but you do need special help."

We continue to reiterate the purpose of the Special Class even after the initial orientation. There is often a great deal of resistance from some children in the first two months of class. One of the most effective ways of overcoming this resistance is to have the "old timers" speak up during a class meeting. A new child may say, "I can leave this class anytime I want to." The student who has been in the class may respond with, "Oh no you can't. You have to stay here until the teacher says you're ready to go. I know." They usually know because they have gone through the same adjustments the previous year. We also go around the circle during class meetings and have the old students say how they felt when they first came to the class and how they feel now.

PARENTAL CONCERNS

Parents have concerns too. Even though the purpose of the Special Class program has been explained by the case psychologist, parents often do not fully understand their child's placement. They, too, are concerned that their child might be in a class for the mentally retarded. For this very reason, we hold a parent orientation meeting as soon as possible. Ideally, we prefer to have parents observe the class prior to the child's placement. At that time, we can usually alleviate some of their fears. There is a definite correlation between the parents' understanding of the placement and the child's acceptance.

FIRST IMPRESSIONS

Some special considerations are brought to bear when a child joins the Special Class after the beginning of the year. First, we prepare the children in class meetings for the new child, get them to talk about what it was like the first time they were in the class, and try to get a volunteer to be a special friend. The new child is best prepared by making one or more visits to the class (which may even occur before the placement decision is made). During these visits, which are usually for an entire day, one can observe strengths and weaknesses, and make initial judgments about why this child may or may not need the class. It's useful to ask for more than one visit by the prospective new student because there is quite a variation in behavior from one visit to the next.

Naturally, what is said in the Special Class forms only a small part of the impression made on the child and the parents. What they see has considerably more impact. Although some parts of the program are more obvious in a single visit than others, most new parents and children report that even on short exposure they pick up an impression of orderliness and control. Structuring both the physical environment and the schedule so as to achieve that sense of orderliness is critical to our program. We amplify on these methods of creating the security a learning disabled child needs in the following chapter.

2

A Time and Place for Everything

Learning disabled children are fragile, insecure individuals, unsure of where they are going and how they are going to get there. These children are easily distracted by their surroundings, confronted by confusion, frightened by the unknown, and discouraged by even small failures. The uncertainty of a learning disabled child's inner personal world makes it necessary for the learning environment to be structured in a predictable fashion. This means that seemingly mundane factors such as how the chairs are arranged, where the paste is located, and how the children enter the classroom are vital aspects for the Special Class. These children have little confidence that they can operate effectively in a complex environment; therefore, we make the environment simple and at first ask them to manage independently only a few behaviors. Remember that nothing can be taken for granted or left to chance—there is a time and place for everything.

Routines for Group Movement and Independent Work

Daily and weekly routines are an important part of a Special Class program and should be carefully established during the first week of school. By providing the children with well-defined structures that tell them how to do things correctly, we help them manage their days so that they always know where they are going. In order to approximate the regular classroom situation as closely as possible, much of the daily program involves the children working and moving in groups. Establishing routines for group movement has two advantages. First, it is easier for us to maintain the learning environment when the children can get from place to place without requiring constant monitoring of each individual. And second, set routines give our children the extra support they need to function responsibly in group situations.

ARRIVING AND DEPARTING PROCEDURES

Repetition is necessary, so every day begins in the same way. The children get off the bus, wait in line while we get a bus report from the driver, and then enter the building together. No one is allowed to run helter-skelter down the hallway. The children are rewarded with crackers or points for correct "coming in" behavior. (For more on rewards for behavior see Chapter 4.) Those who do not follow this simple routine are asked to go back and show us "the right way to do it." Then they are rewarded. Upon entering the classroom, the children put away their coats and lunches, go to the class meeting circle (the chairs are set up ahead of time), and sit down. The class meeting then begins, and with it another school day.

Every day also ends in the same way. When the children have put away all their materials and show us by sitting quietly that they are ready for dismissal, we ask them to stack their chairs on top of their desks and wait until their names are called. When we call their names, the children pick up their lunchpails, coats, and so on, and line up at the classroom door. At that time, we pass out corrected papers and good notes. Then we walk down the hall as a group to board the bus. We say good-bye to each child and wave the bus out of the parking lot.

WORKING IN LEARNING GROUPS

The children are scheduled for group reading, math, language, physical education, and Slingerland phonics. These activities occur at the same time every day. (For the daily schedule see Chapter 3.) We instruct the children at the beginning of the year as to how to move and behave when going from one group to the next. For example, if the children in one group approach their next learning group station and discover that the group in progress has not finished, they have been instructed to stand off to one side in a designated area until the group in progress is excused. The incoming children put their point cards in a specific location, sit down, and are then rewarded by the teacher in charge with points for coming to the group quickly and quietly.

The only period that does change from day to day is the last half hour. This time is variously used for science, social studies, art, music, or a second class meeting if the need arises. This time block follows a short period of ten to fifteen minutes in which the children complete any unfinished independent folder work. We prepare the children for the final activity by setting a timer and saying something like, "I am setting the timer for 10 minutes. When it goes off, please turn in your folders. We will be starting a new art project today in room two." The children are then aware of the kind of activity that will be forthcoming and when, and we are saved from unnecessary time and energy spent in answering a barrage of questions such as "Are we having a movie today?" and "Can't we work on our stitcheries?"

PREPARING FOR RECESSES AND LUNCH

To be excused for recess, the children must be sitting quietly at their desks and all materials must be put away. Then they are dismissed singly or by rows. We ask the children to push in their chairs to help keep the room looking orderly and to prevent other children from stumbling over misplaced furniture. At the end of the day, when the children are excused to go to the bus, we ask them to stack their chairs on top of their desks.

During the first part of the year, the children line up at the door after being excused and we take them out to the playground or to the cafeteria. After they learn the routines for getting to these places (walking, going to the end of the line to get their lunch, and so on), and prove that they can follow the general school rules governing these situations, the children are allowed to go without teacher supervision. Points are awarded for appropriate recess and lunchroom behavior. A child who demonstrates inappropriate recess or lunchroom behavior loses this social privilege for a certain length of time—one day to a week, depending on the severity of the problem. We keep the child in the classroom with some type of on task assignment. This assignment might include the child's completing current folder work, making up missed folder work, or working on a task that reinforces some needed skill. If the lunchroom itself is the trouble spot, we send the child to eat in the classroom and he is excused for recess when the other children in the lunchroom are excused.

We also use lunchroom privileges as a lever with children who consistently waste their independent folder time and don't particularly care if they lose a few points. In other words, no work—no eat. It's amazing how that pencil will fly when the taco aroma is only a few feet away! After the child completes the restriction time, we restate the qualifications for earning lunchroom and recess privileges, involve the child in a discussion of appropriate behavior, and start all over again!

CARRYING CHAIRS

We have found that we must attend to the smallest detail, even to the point of providing the children with a specific method for carrying their chairs. This routine eliminates such games as the "strong man"—holding the chair high overhead hoping to miss everyone else's head in the process; the "train"—lining up two or more chairs, then pushing; and the "potpourri"—pulling, pushing, dragging and getting the chair to its destination regardless of all obstacles in the way. We first label each child's chair with his or her name. When the time comes to move chairs, we tell the children that they are responsible for arriving with their own chairs in an orderly fashion. We also provide the following instructions: "Stand at the side of the chair, grasp the backrest with one hand and the seat with the other hand, lift it off the floor, and carry it ever so gently." Yes, it does save our nerves.

ATTENDING SPECIAL ACTIVITIES

Occasionally the daily schedule changes because of field trips or special events, such as assemblies or cooking projects. We tell the children in advance when changes are going to occur and try to anticipate any problems. For example, a recess might be postponed or learning groups reshuffled. By talking the changes through and, if necessary, charting a new schedule for the day, anxiety is kept at a tolerable level. Sometimes changes happen on the spur of the moment. Our principal unexpectedly invited the class one morning to a band music assembly to be performed by the local high school. We took a few minutes to discuss appropriate behavior at an assembly with the children and then had them line up in an orderly fashion. Once at the cafeteria, we had them sit in a specific place. The brief time spent establishing a routine for attendance paid off with what we considered the most outstanding behavior in the entire audience. Upon returning to the classroom, we went back into the class meeting circle, rewarded the children for their positive behavior, and reset the schedule for the rest of the day.

INDEPENDENT WORK TIME

The daily program should emphasize individual work as well as group participation. When a child works or plays alone during individual time periods, he or she has the opportunity to practice the skills and habits needed for working independently in the regular classroom. Learning disabled children need the guidance of an established routine during these solitary periods to help them successfully function on their own and successfully internalize responsible independent behavior.

Since a learning disabled child often cannot make appropriate choices and accept responsibility for focusing on a task and completing it, it is essential that the teacher guide in the decision making. For example, we structure the independent work time so that the child may choose between working on a math paper first or a written assignment first, but a choice must be made between the two. For some children it is necessary to structure the routine even further. For example, if a child never chooses to do a math paper, then a math paper is paper clipped to the top of the folder and the child must do that paper before any others. We also establish a working order in which any papers needing corrections are paper clipped on top and require top priority.

GETTING TEACHER HELP

Getting teacher help during independent work times is not allowed, but successfully communicating this idea and establishing this routine is one of our most difficult tasks. While some children are working in their learning groups, the rest of the class should be involved in their independent folder work. We take a few minutes right after the morning class meeting, and before the children go to their first learning group, to answer any questions they may have about the papers in their daily folder. Thereafter, they are not allowed to interrupt a teacher working with a group. Hand waving, yelling out "How do you do this?" and eyeballing the teacher nose-to-nose at her teaching station are all ignored. From the beginning, the children are instructed to go on to another paper if they really and truly get stuck. They save the difficult paper for that short period of time in the afternoon when all the teachers are free to help them. Very young children (those coming right out of kindergarten into the Special Class) are a special case and require immediate attention because they often have a limited background in paper and pencil task completion. We sometimes employ sixth grade tutors to assist these young children during their independent folder time.

USING FREE TIME

If a child earns free time, which only occurs when a child either finishes all independent folder work or purchases the time with point cards, he or she can choose a play activity from the free-time shelf. Free-time activities include puzzles, clay work, Leggos, Lincoln Logs, Tinker Toys, and checkers. The children are not allowed to go into the cupboard where the games are stored. The free-time area is separated by a partition so that children still working will not be disturbed. If a child abuses free-time privileges, he or she is sent back to the work area and given a quiet activity for the remainder of the period.

|| Establishing the Physical Environment

The physical environment includes everything in the classroom that the child relates to through the five senses. Everything the child sees, hears, tastes, touches, or smells must have its logical place. We establish the physical surroundings in our Special Class by organizing materials and supplies so that they are ready for use, by keeping visual factors functional and motivational but not distracting, and by providing structured arrangements for all classroom fixtures and furniture.

MATERIALS AND SUPPLIES

Having a structured classroom means that we are always thoroughly prepared to teach reading, math, language, and other curriculum areas each day. This means we have all materials constantly on hand. Because learning disabled students are fearful of surprises in general, a small detail such as not having the paste for an art project may mean the difference between their success and failure. When teaching regular classes, we could send a student off to the storeroom for such an item, but not now! What might seem to be a slight inconvenience can become a major disturbance to one of our students.

The teacher in charge of each learning station organizes all materials needed for her groups. We label folders for individualized worksheets, use makeshift bookcases to store books and workbooks, and keep a supply of primary and other graded writing papers and specialized materials. Supplies are organized right down to the most minute detail. For example, children use red pencils during learning groups and black pencils at their desks, and never the twain shall meet. Because it is not particularly easy for either one of us to remember every detail, we wear a felt pen (to record points) on a yarn necklace, putting it on first thing in the morning and taking it off last thing in the afternoon. (For more on the point system see Chapter 4.)

We store paste, paints, scissors, and paper in the same place all year long. The children are expected to return these supplies to their proper places after use. Not only are we constantly working on getting ourselves better organized, but every endeavor is made to encourage and guide the children in organizing. We feel that the small details such as returning the paste to its proper place starts to build the foundation for responsible behavior.

VISUAL INFLUENCES

Keeping the room uncluttered contributes to maintaining the class's organization and structure. Everything is stored: unused supplies and materials are stored on a high shelf in labeled boxes, moderately used materials are stuffed into cupboards, and frequently used materials are neatly stacked on shelves.

Color is another visual factor that must be considered. One year we moved into two new rooms and half of one room was painted a brilliant orange. Using a color like this anywhere near a Special Class is like waving a red flag in front of a bull. There was only one solution—spend four days prior to the opening of school slapping on a few coats of ecru. Other colors that work advantageously are pastel green, yellow, and off-white. To maintain a consistent color scheme, we permanently cover large bulletin boards with burlap in a shade of tan and border them very simply, with soft yellow construction paper.

This is not to say that the overall scheme should be completely bland. Vibrant colors can be used for various displays, and of course it's a good idea to hang examples of the children's work up on the walls. We always try to have something of merit on exhibit by each child, but we don't hang art work from the rafters and plaster the walls with projects as we did in our regular classrooms.

PHYSICAL ARRANGEMENTS

The classroom itself should present a minimum of distractions but yet avoid being boring. We keep out only a few of the learning centers which are used continuously, plus one task center in each room which is changed frequently. Both classrooms are similar except that the large area used for the class meetings in one room is utilized as a work area in the other. This space has a large table and file cabinets used by our aides to put together the daily individualized independent work folders.

The physical arrangement shown here allows the children free access to all areas with a minimum of distraction to the other children. We strive to place noisy activities away from

Sample Classroom Arrangement

Classroom arrangement provides learning areas both for independent study and for group activity.

quiet learning activities. We make very few changes in the physical arrangement of the classroom during the year.

SEATING FOR DIFFERENT ACTIVITIES

"Everything in its place" includes having *everyone* in his or her place. We use different seating arrangements as different educational needs arise. Tables are usually used for small learning groups. The kidney-shaped adjustable work table works best, for this shape allows up to six children to sit within arms' reach of the teacher and still provides the students with adequate work space and a clear line of vision to the chalkboard.

Learning Group Seating Arrangement

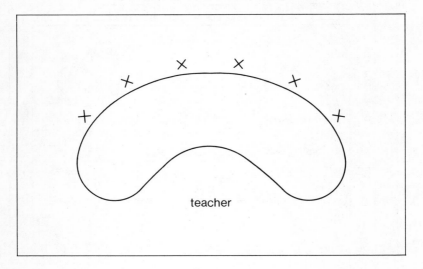

This seating arrangement maximizes the children's chances for attending behavior during small learning group situations.

The children sit at tables while they attend the three learning groups—reading, math, and language. Seating the children at tables allows for maximum attending behavior. We can and do demand eye contact and we can also reach out and touch the children to remind them of our pride in their accomplishments or to refocus their attention. We are close enough in this situation to give immediate tangible rewards for appropriate student behaviors or praise for task completion in the form of stars, happy faces, and so on.

Chairs are placed in a circle formation for large group situations such as daily class meetings, story times, discussions, problem solving sessions, and certain teaching lessons such as science experiments requiring active participation. A circle of chairs is ideal for developing positive listening and communication skills. Each student can make eye contact with everyone else in the group and, in turn, become the center of attention when talking. We require that the children raise their hands to be recognized for a turn, and we ignore spontaneous calling-out. Children are reinforced for looking at another person when they are speaking. It is never too early to begin learning the fine art of listening and developing an interest in what others have to say. (For more on listening and communication skills emphasized in circle meetings see Chapter 4.)

For other large group teaching situations, the children sit at individual desks all facing in the same direction. We have found that the "junior executive" desk style is most efficient. This desk provides an open storage unit for supplies on one side and a rather large flat-top working area to spread out papers. (We suffered through one school year with lift-top desks, which were surely invented as one of the most appealing toys ever made available to learning disabled children. A world's record was set in our class with fifteen "lifts and slams" in a three-minute period!) Individual desks are also used during phonics instruction, art lessons, or any other lesson or project in which the children need to see a chalkboard or require space for manipulating materials. The children sit at their own desks during independent folder time when they work on a variety of paper and pencil tasks. If a child is unable to work at an individual desk stationed in a group setting, the office is an effective alternative.

THE OFFICE

The inability to function in a group is a common problem with learning disabled children. In fact, many of the initial referrals for Special Class placement contain the statement "cannot work in a group situation." This usually means that the child is highly distractible, is unable to complete any assignments, or is continuously disturbing his or her neighbors. During our first year of teaching the Special Classes, we worked with quite a few older children who exhibited these problems. In response to this, we constructed the office, a cubicle made from 5-foot × 4-foot free-standing portable dividers. By pushing these dividers against the walls, we could create twelve offices in an average-sized classroom. Teaching stations are placed in the center of the room.

Plan for Individual "Offices"

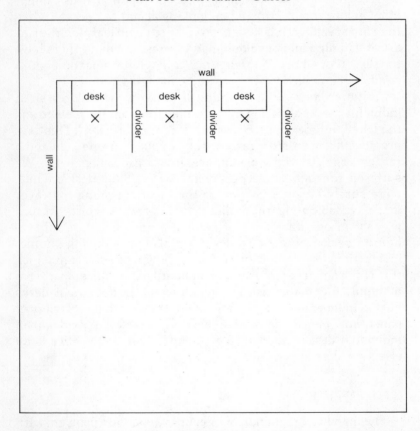

Individual offices give the children places to work away from classroom distractions.

Offices are used both to help children learn how to manage independent work habits and to appreciate being in a group. Being surrounded by walls on three sides and facing a wall places a child in an environment with minimal distractions. Of course, this doesn't mean that an office situation in and of itself will make a child complete assignments or stop yelling out inappropriately. That is the main function of the behavior management system; the office is simply a highly structured physical arrangement which the child cannot leave without permission.

We ignore verbal requests for teacher help that come from an office. When a child is working in an office and needs assistance, a "red flag" is used to signal the teacher. Flags are circular pieces of red and green construction paper stapled together and glued on to a spring type clothespin. The flag is clipped, green side facing out, to the outside edge of one office divider. When the child encounters difficulty, he or she flips the flag to the red side as a signal to the teacher for help. After responding to the signal, the teacher flips the flag back to the green side.

In our experience, the time spent working in the office can range from a short period of time for one child to the entire school year for another. We have found that working with younger children (kindergarten through fourth grade) does not necessitate many sessions in the office. We place a child in an office until we feel the child exhibits the required behavior (attending to tasks, positive social interactions, and so on) necessary for group work. The child earns the right to move back into the mainstream of the classroom when he or she exhibits those behaviors.

3

‖The Day and the Curriculum

We organize our daily classroom program around a consistent time schedule, barring a special activity or an unforeseen crisis. The time blocks in the following schedule are the crucial part:

9:00– 9:10 Children arrive on the bus and come into the room

9:10– 9:40 Class meeting

9:40– 9:45 Question and answer time regarding worksheets in independent folders

9:45–10:05 Learning groups (reading, math, language), or independent folder time

10:05–10:25 Learning groups

10:25–10:45 Learning groups

10:50–11:05 Recess

11:10–11:35 Phonics and physical education. (We teach phonics in one room to half the students while our aides teach physical education in the other room or outside.)

11:35–12:00 Phonics and physical education. (Those students in 11:10 phonics now have physical education and vice versa.)

12:00–12:40 Lunch recess

12:40– 1:00 Storytime. (Aides read a story while we write good notes and get work papers ready to go home.)

1:00– 1:20 Learning groups

1:20– 1:35 Tie up odds and ends from independent folder work

1:35– 2:15 Art, music, social studies, or science

2:20 Dismissal for bus

This time schedule provides the framework for our daily program. It commits us, as much as is humanly possible, to a consistent plan which emphasizes the activities important to developing academic skills. The schedule also allows for the development of social skills and independent work habits, as well as for some enjoyment.

|| Routine Business

THE DAILY CLASS MEETING

Each day begins with a class meeting. During this time, we take care of daily business, provide opportunities for problem solving, and encourage the children to share their experiences and feelings with the group.

The first thing we do in the class meeting is to refer to the helper's chart which hangs on the bulletin board behind the meeting circle. Jobs (lunch tabulator, calendar person, weather person, flag person) are rotated weekly.

LUNCH COUNT

One child is responsible for tabulating the hot lunch count for the cafeteria. This child goes to the front of the group and asks the students who are buying lunch to stand and be counted. The number is recorded on a tally sheet, and then the lunch envelopes are placed on a hook by the door to be picked up by the school secretary. Children who cannot count one-to-one from the center of the circle are instructed to go around the circle and touch each standing child as they count. This tactile reinforcement keeps the lunch count accurate.

CALENDAR REVIEW

Another child is in charge of the calendar review. We have a large masonite calendar equipped with hooks which can be used each month to put up individual dates. We also have a small pocket chart constructed out of tagboard and mounted on the bulletin board which reviews the day's date and other related information. The month cards are printed in red, the days in blue, and the rest of the information in black. The calendar person uses a pointer that hangs next to the pocket chart in

Monthly Calendar

A large, monthly calendar can be used to teach temporal concepts and to record special events.

order to guide the entire group while they recite the information directly from the chart. The calendar person then recites the information. After that, other children are called on to recite the same material individually. The rest of the group is expected to look at the calendar while one person is having a turn. We reward the children with fish crackers or other non-sugar items like pumpkin seeds for attending behavior and for reading the calendar correctly.

The calendar activity is useful for two reasons. First, it teaches the names of the days of the week and the months of the year and second, it provides practice with the concepts of "before and after." For example, a child who cannot recall on Wednesday that the day before was Tuesday, is reminded of the concept of before and after. In addition, the calendar activity requires that the children repeat sentence models that incorporate present, past, and future tenses. We extend this activity's usefulness by repeating the names of the days of the week in rote order as a group. Children volunteer to say the days of the week by themselves, and if successful, their names are recorded on a Days of the Week Club chart. We start a

Tagboard Pocket Chart

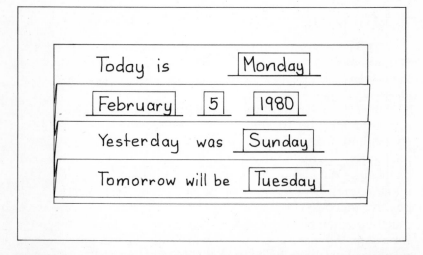

Practicing calendar information helps children to develop temporal concepts.

similar chart for the months of the year after most of the students have successfully recited the days of the week.

The calendar activity also provides an opportunity for students to help each other. Classmates will often rally and help another who is having difficulty mastering this activity. The students will sometimes volunteer to help one another at recess, and we've experienced the group's spontaneous applause when a struggling child correctly remembers the days of the week. It's not long before everyone's name is on the club chart!

WEATHER REPORT

The next activity on the agenda is the weather report. The child assigned as weather person goes to the bulletin board where the weather chart is permanently located. The chart is constructed from tagboard and contains library pockets mounted at the end of each question. Inside each pocket is an index card with a "yes" printed on one side and a "no" on the other side. The question is read by the child assigned as the weather person (with modeling by one of us if the child cannot read), and the appropriate answer exposed (see page 55).

FLAG SALUTE

After the final piece of routine business, the flag person leads the flag salute. We are then ready to move on to a sharing or a problem-solving session. (For more on problem solving in the class meeting see Chapter 4.)

Officially beginning the day with the class meeting has proven invaluable. It sets a positive and open tone for the day. By beginning the day with familiar material, students experience success early in the day. We discuss and reach solutions for problems which may have developed at home or on the bus while coming to school. This clears the air and establishes a positive mood. A child cannot think about the mechanics of two plus two when all that he or she wants to do is knock someone for a loop. We make every possible attempt to conclude the class meeting only when each child is in control of his or her own personal situation and is ready to begin working in the daily learning groups.

|| Remedial Small Group Instruction

Just prior to beginning the daily learning groups, we have a five minute question and answer period. The children look through their independent assignments and ask questions on any paper or task they don't understand. We answer their questions and then move on to the first learning group. These groups are the setting for our remedial program, and in the following sections we share some of the materials and techniques we have found to be especially useful. To some extent, these various approaches are an expression of what we prefer to do as teachers individually. No teacher functions well doing something that doesn't suit his or her style. And so the approach varies somewhat depending on which one of us is using it.

READING INSTRUCTION

How we wish we had all the magical answers to teaching reading, since this one area creates more frustration to learning disabled children than any other. The process begins by conducting a fairly detailed study of the child's test results and past records to determine whether his or her strength lies in the auditory, visual, or kinesthetic area, or in a combination thereof. Sometimes the answer is obvious when we take a quick glance at the child's reading instruction history. The records might reveal three years of using a basic sight approach and the fact that the child couldn't get beyond the second preprimer level. This tells us that the main instructional method being used was probably in the child's area of greatest weakness. Either that, or the teachers were not conscious of modality differences or were unaware of how to handle them. This used to be the case more than it is now; now we often find that a teacher has focused consciously on remediating a weakness, and overemphasized that method of instruction.

We're prone to fall into the same error. It *is* hard to push that weakness into the background, and it is easy to think "Oh my God, I've got to help Henry hear the differences in sounds, even if it takes me all year." Unfortunately, that approach may leave Henry still reading on the second preprimer level at the end of the year. And if his weakness is profound in that area, he still may not be able to hear the difference between *b* and *d*. When teaching reading, we always concentrate on the child's strong learning modality, and try to alleviate the weakness when we can find the time to do so.

After we have done our own testing to determine individual learning strengths and current reading instructional levels, we group each child with one to three other children who fit into the same category. Naturally, this doesn't work out into eight

Tagboard Weather Chart

Is the sun shining ?	yes
Is it a cloudy day ?	no
Is it a rainy day ?	no
Is the wind blowing ?	no
Is it cold outside ?	no
Is it warm outside ?	yes

Giving a weather report develops an awareness of the environment and provides practice in reading and in reasoning.

neat groups of three each. Some reading groups may consist of a group of one. Incidentally, many people think that Special Classes should be individualized on a one-to-one basis. We do plan children's programs individually, but there is a great deal of benefit to creating compatible small groups for instruction. Both teacher and student benefit—teacher preparation time is decreased, and the student is exposed to more instruction and to the values inherent in belonging to a group.

The materials and approaches we use are much the same as would be found in a cross section of regular classrooms: basal readers (most are still slanted to strong visual learners), linguistic readers that are used both linguistically and with a sound-blending approach (most often the *Merrill Linguistic Readers*); phonetic readers (several series are available from Educator's Publishing Service); and language experience for poorly motivated, kinesthetic learners.

In our experience, it is most difficult to teach the kinesthetic learner who has both severe auditory and visual perceptual problems. One method we've used successfully has been to write simple books that revolve around the child's interests—animals, motorcycles, trucks, and so on. These books incorporate a limited vocabulary that contains both phonetic and sight words. To assemble this vocabulary we make word boxes (a recipe file box with 3 × 5 index cards) which are then utilized for word study. The child traces the word, writes it on the chalkboard, paints it at the easel, and types it. All of these multisensory (and strongly kinesthetic) techniques help commit that word to memory.

A singular approach, though, is not enough for a learning disabled child. What makes the difference is a persistent, day in and day out reinforcement that uses a lot of different materials in a variety of ways. An example of this is the way we start each reading group with word study. Each child has a manila envelope that contains flashcards, each one of which has a word written on it. The source for the flashcards varies according to individual needs. Some children may be working on a letter recognition, others on basic sight words from the Dolch List, and still others on words from their readers. A mark is made on the back of the card if the child can say the word without any prompting from the teacher. When a card contains ten marks, we consider the word mastered, and it is set aside for occasional review. Just seeing the mark made by the teacher appears to be reinforcement in itself. The children themselves create games centering around work study—how many words they have mastered, when they will get new words, and how many more marks until mastery. All of the cards are kept at school until the end of the year, at which time they are sent home for summer review.

After word study, the group proceeds to other activities such as presentation of new vocabulary, silent and oral reading, word attack skills, and comprehension skills. This is a good time to jot down pertinent observations about individual children (for example, confusing *want* and *went*) so that appropriate follow-ups can be instituted.

Reinforcement

Some of the follow-up multisensory reinforcement methods well received by the children are:

- **Typing.** Depending on a child's current functional level, he or she is given a worksheet in the independent folder consisting of either letters, words, or sentences. The instructions indicate how many times the exercise is to be typed; the child then reads the typing paper to an instructor. This activity is very popular with the students.

- **Painting.** The child is given a sheet of paper with an appropriate word, phrase, or sentence printed on it. The student then reads the exercise to an instructor, copies it on the same paper, and paints a picture to match the exercise. Not only does this activity reinforce reading vocabulary, but it also works on eye-hand coordination, fine-motor skills, and body image, since many of the exercises are about the children themselves. Perhaps the most enjoyable aspect of this activity is the painting itself.

- **Tracing.** We use a variety of materials for tracing activities including crayons, paints, watercolors, chalk, sand, glue, yarn, clay, and tracing paper. (For a free supply of tracing paper use the protection sheet that's placed between ditto masters.) Children do not tire of tracing the same word over and over if the teacher provides a wide and imaginative variety of materials.

Other useful resources for reading reinforcement materials are:

Elwell, Murray, and Kucia, *Phonics Workbooks*. Cleveland, Ohio: Modern Curriculum Press, rev. ed. 1980.

Makar, Barbara W., *Primary Phonics Workbooks*. Cambridge, Mass.: Educator's Publishing Service, 1966–1977.

Welles, Anne L. and Eleanor D. Griffin, *Sound Off*. Cambridge, Mass.: Educator's Publishing Service, 1973–1976.

Program Planning

The important thing to remember when using any material is to make sure it fits the needs of the child. We don't recommend automatically starting on page one of the workbook and continuing along in numerical order because a child's instructional level and needs may not match the workbook's order. What we do is tear apart the books, and reorganize materials to fit each child's skills and level. If Sally is working on the sound of the letter *s*, then we go through her materials and locate all the appropriate *s* worksheets.

Some basic points about program planning are worth mentioning here. Caution is always advised when you want to move a child to another learning level. Children are often placed beyond their true instructional level to start with, and we usually start "way back," to allow them to fill in missing skills. When those skills appear to have been mastered, it's always tempting to move them up right away. But if we go too fast, we are likely to place the child back into the same frustration of not being able to do the work from which he or she has just escaped. Often it's better to continue with more horizontal movement— that is, working on the same level.

It is also wise to assess a child's achievement of independent usage of a skill very carefully. For most children learning to read, judging independence is a fairly simple matter, but this isn't the case with most learning disabled children. They usually need many reinforcements of a skill before it can be reliably and independently applied.

PHONICS INSTRUCTION

Each child receives about 25 minutes of daily instruction with specialized phonics methods devised by Beth H. Slingerland. But we present letters and sounds in the sequence found in *Recipe for Reading* by Nina Traub (see page 154). The Slingerland techniques involve the auditory, visual, and kinesthetic modalities. We use this method to teach the sound-symbol relationships of the letters of the alphabet, manuscript and cursive letter formation, sound blending, and dictation skills.

It is not possible to give a detailed account of the Slingerland approach here. However, training courses are available throughout the United States during the summer. Manuals with auxiliary materials are available from Educator's Publishing Service. We recommend this approach because it really works. When children have deficits in one or more of the three learning channels—auditory, visual, or kinesthetic—our experience shows that training them in a highly structured, sequential reading and language arts program (such as the Slingerland method) produces the best results. The children develop very specific strategies for memory and representation, which seem to compensate effectively for their disabilities. We firmly believe in the Slingerland method, but we are also aware that our enthusiasm for it may increase its effectiveness for us.

MATH INSTRUCTION

After we establish the instructional level of each child, we then set up an individualized program that incorporates as many different types of activities as possible. These activities rely heavily on manipulative materials such as counters, blocks, bean sticks, Cuisinaire rods, individual clocks, play money, clock and money stamps (which are highly motivational and available from most educational catalogs and teacher supply shops), matrices, and number lines. The manipulative materials are used to aid the children in understanding and completing regular math workbooks. Just as we do with reading materials, we organize the math workbooks to fit each individual's needs and instructional level, marking up or tearing out pages as needed.

Sometimes understanding the concept behind a mathematical operation is not possible for a learning disabled child, and so we don't worry about teaching those concepts. We're more concerned with providing the child with the necessary skills to function mathematically in our society. We want the children to learn the four basic computational skills of addition, subtraction, multiplication, and division. If a child cannot recall the basic facts prerequisite to implementing these skills, we have no qualms about permanently providing him or her with a multiplication table or similar aid. If we work with older children experiencing similar retention problems, a calculator is in order. Again, we emphasize the child's strengths rather than his or her weaknesses.

Telling time and making change are the two areas we cover extensively in our math program. Assignments in these topics are tailored to the individual child and reinforcement is consistently provided in the independent folder assignments. A few high-interest activities in this area include: clock and time worksheets, money counting exercises, money tasks involving counting and making change, and tasks involving rubber stamps, clock-face stamps, and play money.

PHYSICAL EDUCATION INSTRUCTION

Most educators are aware of the need for developing children's physical skills. Before we implemented a physical education program in our regular classroom, we felt uneasy about the fact that we had not made physical education an important part of our daily program. When we became Special Class teachers, it became obvious that the lack of sensory-motor integration in our students made a physical education program absolutely necessary. The physical education program we developed is designed around basic physical skills—walking, running, rolling, jumping, hopping, skipping, leaping, sliding, catching, throwing, and so on. We use materials and equipment such as hoola hoops, small rubber balls, jump ropes, exercise mats, and a parachute. Simple, minimal competition games are taught to reinforce the skills.

In our opinion, one of the most exciting results of continuing to develop our physical education program has been the inclusion of yoga as part of the daily routine. (Our aides asked if they could take a special course in teaching yoga to young children, and we freed them to do so.) As a result, we began using some of the relaxation exercises at other times besides the regular physical education period. For example, after a particularly tense discussion during a class meeting, we instruct everyone to assume a sitting relaxation position for one minute. It really helps! After the relaxation exercise, the children are ready to attend to a task or to move on to the next activity.

During physical education the children practice a variety of yoga postures that aid in improving body awareness and control. Parents were very impressed when the children put on a yoga demonstration at one open house. Books on teaching yoga to young children are available at most bookstores and public libraries. One that is particularly useful is Rachael Carr's *Yoga For All Ages,* New York: Simon and Schuster.

We use so many other kinds of physical education activities in our program that it is not feasible to list them all. Rather, we feel that it's more helpful to list the resources we have used most extensively in our classrooms:

Alameda County School Department. *The Development of Basic Motor Skills.* Hayward, California: Alameda County School Department, 1968.

Belgau, Frank. *A Perceptual-Motor and Visual Perception Handbook of Developmental Activities.* Port Angeles, Wash.: Perception Development Research Associates, 1971.

Capon, Jack, and Hallum, Rosemary. *Perceptual Motor Rhythm Games.* (record and manual) Freeport, New York: Educational Activities, 1973.

De Santis, Gabriel, and Smith, Lester. *ERCAPEP—Physical Education Program Guide for Grades K–6.* Columbus, Ohio: Charles E. Merrill, 1969.

Hackett, Layne, and Jensen, Robert. *Guide to Movement Exploration.* Palo Alto, California: Peek Publications, 1973.

Mullane, Jack. *Keep on Steppin'.* (record) Freeport, New York: Educational Activities, Inc., 1975.

Seker, JoAnn, and Jones, George. *Parachute Play.* (record and manual) Freeport, New York: Educational Activities, Inc., 1969.

MUSIC, ART, SOCIAL STUDIES, AND SCIENCE

We approach these areas on a theme level, and try to cover three out of the four areas in each theme. Typical themes are "Our Community," "Animals," or "Health." We attempt to conduct an activity in one of these areas every day. Sometimes it's difficult fitting everything in, even on a weekly basis. One art project may go on for several days. If a big problem arises it may be necessary to hold a second class meeting during this time. Since the age span in a Special Class varies so much, materials must be designed which are at a low enough level to have meaning for the youngest child but at a high enough level to appeal to the older, more able child. The following is a brief example of a unit that incorporates science, social studies, and art, all revolving around the sun as the theme.

We begin by viewing simple filmstrips concerning scientific facts about the sun, picking and choosing the frames to be seen. Then, as part of the follow-up discussion, we construct large charts, listing the information in the children's vocabulary. These charts go up on the walls so they can be reviewed as needed. The children also start notebooks containing "sun words" plus facts on shadows, energy, and how the sun supports life. The art projects are stimulated by a film depicting the symbol of the sun in art. Various projects might include a sunburst shape made from paper plates that have been covered with colorful tissue paper; clay sunbursts mounted on plywood which the children have sanded, stained, and varnished; sunburst designs permanently enshrined on plastic plates; and suns stitched with burlap yarn in a vast array of colors and original designs. Other units we have successfully developed for learning disabled children have centered around plants, animals, whales, our city, map reading, and self and family.

There just isn't enough time during the day to give all curriculum areas equal treatment. Every curriculum is important, but the high priority for learning disabled children is to develop their academic skills. There remains one subject, however, that we have not yet covered—language. Its importance permeates every other learning group and is central to the whole educational process.

LANGUAGE AND COMMUNICATION

There is a specific time in our daily program for language instruction. At this time, the children participate in the usual language arts disciplines, such as handwriting, phonics reinforcement, and creative writing. In addition to these activities, the aide in charge of the language group spends time working with the younger children on language development. We generally employ the *Peabody Language Development Kits* and the *Wilson Syntax Program* because they both provide an easy-to-follow sequence of presentation, in addition to having all the necessary materials for carrying out the lessons. The older children that don't need oral language development work on keeping journals, writing class newspapers, and creating poetry. The language program emphasizes both oral and written expression.

However, teaching language does not end with language time. Since many learning disabled children have severe deficits in receptive and expressive language skills, the teacher should maintain an awareness of language's central role in learning throughout the entire day. For example, we occasionally tape record the language used by the children during the class meeting. Recording language has proven to be an efficient tool for use in evaluating the children's language needs, as well as providing a record of who participates in what way.

We recommend using the following techniques to improve receptive and expressive language skills in both individual and group activities:

- **Asking for feedback.** After directions have been given, ask specific children to repeat them back—"Larry, what are you going to do now?"
- **Giving increasingly difficult directions.** We begin with one direction, "Larry, please get your pencil." We then add a related direction to the original, "Larry, please get your pencil and come to the math table." We expand the direction to include up to three and four tasks, "Larry, please get your pencil, come to the math table, and open your book. . . ." With some children it may be necessary to

use the feedback technique after each direction is given. Many learning disabled children become highly confused when they are given a whole string of verbal directions, and are simply unable to follow them. Teachers often misinterpret this behavior as purposely not following directions, but it's usually a case of simply not understanding the directions.

- **Teaching abstract language concepts.** The Boehm Test of Basic Concepts can be useful at this state in pinpointing specific deficits. However, many learning disabled children have problems in this area. So we make a concentrated effort to teach these concepts by providing generalized worksheets, such as one that contains several geometric shapes. (Before handing the children this kind of worksheet, first make sure they can identify basic geometric shapes!) Directions are given—"Put an X on the circle; put an X above the square; put an X under the triangle." After each direction check that each child understands. If there is confusion, involve the children in an activity that helps to clarify the concept. For example, if the children have trouble marking the figure located between two others, we have three children come to the front of the room to demonstrate the concept "between." We give oral directions such as "Mario, please stand between Michelle and Jack. Now, Jack, stand between Mario and Michelle."

- **Insist on complete sentences.** If the child attempts to answer a question with one word or a simple phrase, we require him or her to use a complete sentence. We may have to model it or at least begin the sentence again for the child. For example, the question is asked, "How do you feel when the sun is shining?" Mark says, "Good." The prompt "tell me in a whole sentence" may be sufficient to get a better response. If not, say "Repeat after me, I feel. . . ." and have Mark finish it.

- **Building vocabulary.** We continually define words for the children until we are satisfied that they understand the meanings. When we encounter a new word, we have the students repeat the word after us as a group. We then ask individual students to repeat the word and give a definition for it. If a child incorporates a new word into his or her speaking vocabulary, we lavish a lot of positive reinforcement on the child in front of the other children.

The different kinds of language development activities presented here are not occasional lessons in our program. They take place every day. Learning disabled children often need frequent repetition of a concept before it is assimilated. We cannot assume that, having demonstrated the concept "over" on one day, that Larry will be able to put the X over the circle on the next day. Each day's program builds on the experiences of the previous day, while also laying the groundwork for the next.

INDEPENDENT FOLDER WORK

The children have one period every day in which they are not directly supervised by an adult. This period is their independent folder time. During this period, the children are expected to complete the assignments in their folder *without teacher assistance.* With this kind of activity we are teaching the kids to conquer their tendency to depend on us, through independent work. They must learn how to make their own decisions on task understanding, completion, and priorities.

In addition to reading reinforcement materials and math follow-up activities, each child's folder contains the following:

- **Individualized spelling contracts.** We provide four activities that the child can read and a summary test to check mastery of the words.

- **Visual-motor worksheets.** We use a variety of sources. They include such activities as design completion, design copying, outlining shapes, and tracing patterns.

- **Tracking worksheets.** Excellent material is available from commercial sources such as the *Michigan Tracking Program,* edited by Donald Smith, Ann Arbor Publishers, Ann Arbor, Michigan. We also use teacher-made dittos and pages from magazines with directions such as "Find the *d*s and find the word *saw.*"

- **Task assignments.** We employ task assignments to involve the child in multisensory activities and to reinforce skills in all subject areas. Task assignments might include a listening center task—listening with a headset to a story and completing a follow-up activity such as painting a picture to demonstrate comprehension of the story or answering a simple question on the story; story sequencing with pictures, cartoons, and sentences; puzzles; word and picture matching exercises; and reproducing patterns with geoboards, pegboards, parquetry tiles, and design blocks. Upon completion of a task, the child leaves the task assignment sheet in the assigned center area, which indicates the task is complete. We then check the assignment at the end of the learning group time.

At the end of the folder work period, we check each child's folder work, award appropriate behavior points, and record the points on the children's point cards. (For more on point cards see Chapter 4.)

Folder time is important to our program. It helps the child assume responsibility for his or her own work and behavior, and is good preparation for the expectations usually encountered in a regular classroom. How the child behaves during folder time is a fairly accurate indication of his or her ability to cope with somewhat unstructured time.

|| Field Trips to Broaden Experience

There usually isn't much classroom time available for social studies, science, or other subjects which are above and beyond the necessary work in remediating basic skills, so we try to take as many field trips as possible throughout the year. They give us a basis for classroom discussions on a fresh topic, and often can be arranged to tie in with the social studies or science units we do manage.

Regardless of whether we take the children two blocks away to the post office or twenty miles away to a concert, behavioral standards are firmly established before anyone leaves the classroom. Several class meetings include instructions on proper car or bus behavior, manners when other people are speaking, staying with the group, and such basics as appropriate clothing and proper lunches. The consequence for inappropriate behavior is reviewed several times prior to a trip, too—a child who cannot manage his or her own behavior is not allowed to attend the next trip. Instead, we make arrangements with a regular classroom teacher for the child to remain at school with a packet of work. Our experience has shown that at least one child will test the limits of our first field trip. After that, things generally go smoothly.

Our initial trips are walking excursions within the community to the fire station, police station, post office, library, or park for flying kites. As we become outward bound, we search for places that will enrich the limited experiences of many of our children.

Other places we recommend taking children are:
- Local aquarium and Academy of Sciences
- Specialized gardens
- Local park to watch spring flowering (we have a picnic and paint watercolor pictures of the cherry trees)
- Specialized museums geared to children's interests
- Historic sites
- Contemporary points of interest
- Hikes with an eye to the local ecological features
- Cultural performances such as children's ballet

Field trips are followed by school discussions, group chart stories, murals, paintings, individual stories typed and dittoed with enough copies for everyone, group letters of appreciation to special guides, and stories written by the children about photographs taken on the trip. All of these activities help the learning disabled child crystallize the experience and broaden his or her own horizons.

But, no matter how often we provide new experiences or expand the scope of learning, the whole process is impossible without behavior guidelines. Our daily program is dependent on an effective behavior management system, to be discussed in Chapter 4.

4

Helping Children Manage Their Behavior

Whether it is a special education classroom or a regular classroom, effective and successful teaching depends on that elusive element commonly known as discipline or classroom control. You can have the latest and most expensive materials, know every child's reading and math level, and individualize or group the children for instruction, arrange the classroom and furniture into every possible configuration, and spend endless hours making learning centers, but it doesn't mean a thing if you find yourself spending the majority of the school day telling the children to *stop it*.

Teacher education classes used to outline those discipline techniques that were not advisable in the modern classroom (rapping knuckles, and so on), and there were vague references to intrinsic motivation as opposed to extrinsic motivation. But we were left to discover intrinsic motivation on our own. We have worked out a number of ways of working with children and helping *them* to assume responsibility for their own behavior. But we prefer to talk about behavior management and self-control, concepts that go beyond what is usually meant by discipline.

Discipline implies force from the outside, force which must be constantly present to maintain its effect. At first, we do exert an outside force on the child to inhibit nonattending and disruptive behaviors, and to encourage the child to assume attending behaviors, but we reduce this force as soon as the child begins to display positive behavior. The goal of our behavior management system is to build the child's self-esteem so that he can take responsibility for his own behavior. We exhibit consistency, fairness, and a willingness to listen, and bolster self-esteem by showing the children that someone does care for them as individuals. At the same time, however, we convey the explicit message that self-respect is gained through self-control. We emphasize that the child's task is to take charge of his or her own life.

|| The Stages of Our Approach

Our behavior management system is founded on three convictions: that the behavior we want a child to show must be very clearly defined for the child and for us; that we must all (teachers and children) keep those behaviors in mind amidst the other activities of the day; and, that our communication about successes and failures needs to be clear, immediate, and supportive of the entire child, not just of the "child who is practicing how to sit still and attend." We achieve the goal of defining specific behaviors by observing children very carefully, and discussing among ourselves which basic actions of theirs are functional and which dysfunctional. We achieve the second through a charting and rewards system that makes progress very evident to the child, and keeps the specific behavior or behaviors desired constantly in view. We achieve the third goal by staying closely in touch with each other as a team, and recognizing both the limitations and benefits of our charts and rewards. Staying in touch with each other about the children helps us keep our expectations consistent and also lets the children know we are all working together toward the same goals.

MINIMUM ACCEPTANCE BEHAVIOR

When we start with a new child (or have a largely new group), we first concentrate on very basic behaviors. Usually with a new child, this phase only lasts the first three or four weeks of the school year. As our experience with learning disabled children has increased over the years, we have become steadily more insistent on controlled and standard behaviors of certain kinds. For example, we have defined exactly how chairs are to be carried safely, how children are to sit in a chair correctly, and how they are to assume a "listening position." ("Listening position" indicates that the child is to sit straight, hands at rest, feet flat on the floor, with his or her eyes making facial contact with the teacher or other person speaking.) Over the years, we have noticed a direct correlation between a child's posture (position and movements of hands, feet, and head) and how well a child listens. Therefore we reward this behavior frequently during learning group periods, and particularly at the beginning of the year.

The behavior of getting into listening position (and other similar behaviors) is important also in terms of the other behaviors it makes impossible. With learning disabled children, these are primarily avoidance or withdrawal behaviors. The child who is twirling his hair, twisting his shirt collar, rubbing his belly, or leaning back in his chair is siphoning off energies into that activity to keep from doing a task felt as threatening or difficult. These behaviors are a serious obstruction to learning as well as a serious threat to the child's overcoming his or her other disabilities.

In order to focus children's attention on one behavior we want them to learn (such as the listening position), we initially use the star chart. The behavior is clearly indicated on the chart, and there is space for a visual reward (stick-on stars) for each period during the day. (The recess columns are an extra, and are used to add stars for more generally positive behavior during those free times.) The child using a star chart carries it from activity to activity, and the teacher in charge of that activity looks at the chart when the child enters to be reminded of the desired behavior. Then the teacher evaluates the child's performance during that period, and adds a star if the behavior was exhibited. The teacher also notes problems that have occurred such as refusal to work or a "time-out" (described on pages 80–81) on the chart. These notations serve as our record for the day, since each teacher in turn can quickly review the child's previous performance. The chart goes home with the child periodically to keep the parents informed as well.

In the star chart phase, a child is working with only one behavior at a time. Usually, we've found that a child needs to work on a single behavior for a maximum of two weeks. If the desired behavior is shown consistently during the beginning of the second week we may stop that week's star chart at that point. Learning two behaviors with the star chart system is typical for a beginning child. Then that child is ready to join the general group in practicing the five general behaviors we stress the entire year.

THE TARGET BEHAVIORS

At or near the beginning of the school year we identify, and begin to work on, the following target behaviors with the children:

- To come to each learning group or other activity quietly, and to not disturb the other people in the classroom
- To get right to work in each learning group
- To be kind to others
- To follow directions from teachers
- To complete work neatly and accurately

These five target behaviors were chosen for two reasons. First, both child and teacher can easily observe the behaviors and also identify more specific actions that either fit within them or don't. The child can readily see that they are functional and "right." Second, all the behaviors help the child become a cooperative member of a group, and when each child is demonstrating all five fairly consistently, the learning environment works.

The first stage of promoting the target behaviors is to identify positive actions already employed by the children and to call attention exclusively to them, both to reinforce the child and to set them up as models for the other children to imitate. (This is done to a greater degree when there are more new students.) An example is a child walking down the hall without crashing into anyone, a child hanging his or her coat on the hook rather than throwing it on the floor, or a child carrying a chair to a class meeting correctly. Immediate praise and small tokens such as pretzels or crackers are the rewards. We state exactly the behavior we are rewarding to the group. For example, "Sally, I like the way you are sitting," "Phil, you really know how to wait for your turn to talk," or "Frank, you raised your hand for a turn. That's good." As time goes on, the rewards are less frequent, and also as time goes on, we ask other children to tell us why a particular child was rewarded. Within a few weeks, we have taught the children what we define as positive behaviors and established the structure of the classroom in the process.

Behavior Star Chart

Sammy is working on listening position
Week of September 10-14

	Reading	Language	Math	First Recess	P.E.	Slinger-land	Lunch Recess	Folder Time
Mon.	☆	.☆	☆	☆	☆		☆	☆
Tues.								
Wed.								
Thurs.								
Fri.								

The star chart is used to shape one basic desired behavior.

Rewards and positive feedback aren't particularly novel. What is somewhat unusual is our tactic of focusing almost entirely on these positive behaviors, regardless of how ordinary they may be. It is usually the case that Christopher, who meticulously crashes and bangs his way into a meeting, gets all the attention. Everyone watches *him*, laughs at *him*, makes comments about *him*, and the teacher reprimands *him*. Thomas, though, comes up quietly without incident and is unnoticed. Breaking this pattern, we have found, requires extreme concentration, but by totally ignoring a Christopher, the situation is turned around, and the child who is trying so hard to do the right thing is complimented and reinforced.

POINT CARDS: SYSTEMATIC REWARD FOR THE TARGET BEHAVIORS

When our focus on the positive is solidly established (again, the time varies with the proportion of new children in the group), we introduce point cards, our device for keeping the target behaviors highlighted for the children. The cards are not only reminders of the desired behaviors, but hold the reward for success with them, and keep all the adults in touch with the child's performance on an hour-by-hour basis.

A sample card is shown on page 75. Each space records both a point *and* the behavior for which it was earned. Children carry their cards with them to each separate learning group or activity, and each teacher in charge of that group or activity fills spaces with the number code of the behavior successfully shown during that activity. On the point card shown, Bill showed all five target behaviors during his first learning group, but didn't get right to work in the second, failed to get right to work or to be kind in the third, but displayed all five behaviors again in the fourth. Note that the "boundary" between activities is marked with a wide mark. This is done at the beginning of each day. Each teacher or aide adds this mark right after the final number is added as a signal to the next teacher seeing the card to start at that point.

It's evident that each card contains a lot of information about the child's behavior, and eventually that information gets home to the parents. But prior to that, the completed cards become

Behavior Point Card

Points for ___Bruce___
Date started ___Oct. 10___
completed _____

1	2	3	4	5	1	3	4	5	1
3	4	1	2	3	4	5			

Good
for you!

1 = comes to group quietly
2 = gets right to work
3 = is kind to others
4 = listens and follows directions
5 = completes work accurately and neatly

Recorded numbers indicate acceptable behaviors during learning groups and recesses. Dark divider indicates a change of learning group.

the basis of a reward system in the class. They become currency of a sort, usable for purchases or privileges. The system works as follows:

Completed cards are deposited in the "bank" in a savings account. The bank is a box divided into sections—one section for each child's account. Every Friday afternoon we open the bank for withdrawals so that the students can claim their point cards and purchase prizes from the "store" if they choose to do so. We formalize this "banking and purchasing" period. The children sit in a circle. We ask each child in turn if he or she wants to spend point cards for store prizes on that day. We withdraw the point cards from the bank for the children who decide to purchase prizes. After each child has a turn to decide whether or not to spend point cards, we open the store for the buyers. (We display store items on a large bulletin board and cover the contents with a curtain when the store is closed.)

The store contains a variety of prizes available for different prices. For one point card, a child can buy a piece of sugarless bubble gum; a box of raisins; a pass for ten minutes free time to play a game of their choice; ten minutes of painting at the easel; permission to take a puzzle home overnight; a pass to go to lunch three minutes early for two days; or a pass for three drinks of water at anytime during the day. The last item is very popular and grew out of the numerous requests for water throughout the day and our consequent reluctance to let them interrupt learning groups with trips to the water fountain. Now that the privilege is earned, both children and teachers are happier. The child presents the pass to the teacher in charge as a signal for a drink of water. The teacher then initials the pass as a record of how many drinks have been taken.

For two or more cards we sell bean bags, erasers, pencils, crayons, felt pens, and colored paper. Some of our most expensive items include animal posters and Matchbox cars, costing ten cards each. In order to get the store going as a motivator, we open it immediately when the first child in the class fills the first point card. Thereafter in the first two or three months, openings are fairly frequent. As the newness wears off, children learn to save their cards for bigger prizes, and the store is open less frequently. But we occasionally have a "Grand Opening" with all the class members present to ooh and ahh when a child who has been saving toward a high-priced item finally completes the last card needed to buy it. The system works best when we listen for the children's clues as to what rewards are most desired at a given time.

INDIVIDUALIZING THE CRITERIA

It should be said that all the adults involved cooperatively set, and keep each other informed of, the detailed criteria for giving each child the point for a particular behavior. For example, one child might be given credit for "being kind to others" if he or she refrains from hitting other children during an activity or learning group period. Another child might be required to interact positively with other children during that time. Children with severe motor problems should not be expected to exhibit the same standards of neatness or quickness as those without motor problems.

|| The Good Note

When a child has an outstanding day, which means that he was cooperative in the learning groups and exhibited self-control during recesses and in the cafeteria as well as in the class, we attach a written note to his daily take-home papers. This is the "good note," which is intended to reinforce the child's feeling of accomplishment with his parents as well as with us and the class. It seems to function on a different and more powerful level than the tangible rewards of stars, points, and store purchases, and has been one of the most uniformly successful parts of our behavior management system.

Initially, the note is easy to earn, but we steadily increase our expectations thus challenging the child to continue to improve behavior. Every week we discuss our expectations with the children individually during our class meetings. For example, we may say to Barry, "You are having trouble getting your folder work done. Do you feel that there is too much? Are you wasting time during that period? Your good note will depend on you finishing your folder every day on time. You will also have to be cooperative during the rest of the day." Or perhaps Sandra is involved in teasing and name-calling. We may simply tell her, "Sandra, we have talked about the name-calling in class meetings with you and with the other children involved. We do not feel that there has been enough improvement. To get a good note, you must not tease or call other people names."

Sample "Good Note"

The good note reinforces a child's positive behavior for that day.

A glance at each child's star charts or point cards allows us to make very specific comments as we present the notes at the end of a day. The comments are always praise for a particular behavior, which adds to the impact of the note. Typical comments are: "Jim, you really worked on listening today," or "Peter, you sure worked hard in reading. We really think it's great how well you're doing."

The child who has earned a good note is excused early and allowed to walk down the hall and to the bus on his or her own since responsible behavior has been demonstrated throughout the entire day. After leaving class, the children in our classes usually head directly for the principal's office where they receive congratulations, stickers for their notes, hugs, some friendly words of encouragement, and even signed comments on the notes.

Parents are key figures in making the good note work, and they must be informed of its meaning early in the year. The good note is a major topic in our first orientation meeting of the year, which is usually scheduled for the first week of school. At this meeting, which is reviewed in more detail in Chapter 5, we tell the parents that the note is a frequent (sometimes daily) communication to keep them informed on the child's progress toward particular behaviors. They are not necessarily the same as the target behaviors discussed on pages 72–74. The good notes are used to reinforce a specific behavior or an honest attempt to do what we ask even though that attempt may not meet with complete success. We explain these behaviors to parents in more detail in individual conferences and frequent phone calls throughout the school year. We also stress to the parents that good notes are difficult to earn and that the children have to work hard for them. We emphasize that the good note offers parents the chance to become personally involved in a positive way with their child's work at school. We ask parents whose children are continuing with us from the previous year to talk about how they have found ways to make the note important at home. Some parents have set up special rewards that can be earned by a given number of notes. We also stress that the children should not be punished if they do not bring home a note. If there is a serious problem they'll hear about it with a phone call; and if not, they can rest assured that we're encouraging the kind of behavior that may earn a note the next day.

Finally, we share our experiences with the parents and remind ourselves that the good note helps us keep the whole child in perspective. As we have already said, the charts sometimes lead us to perceive a child strictly from the viewpoint of a desired behavior being worked on at a particular time. We need to guard against that excess. Our commitment to issue a large number of good notes fairly frequently keeps us on the lookout for whatever strength and positive behavior a child may exhibit, as well as those we are specifically encouraging.

|| The Time-Out

When a child loses control, we send him or her on a time-out. A time-out allows the child time to cool down and also reinforces the principle that no one has the right to violate the rights of others through a loss of control. We consider a loss of control to include the following behaviors: physical assault; excessive swearing; refusal to follow directions or work within the class structure; self-destructive emotional outbursts, such as pounding on the desk; rocking and talking to avoid an assigned task; or refusing to stop talking about an incident that happened at recess and that has already been discussed. With such losses of control, we send the child away from the group on a time-out.

The time-out provides the necessary time for a child to regain control over his or her own behavior. The child is sent to an area where there is as little visual and auditory stimulation as possible. This area may be the vacated nurse's room in the office or an alcove in an unused hallway. Ideally, it would be a small room built into a corner of the classroom. Once stationed in the time-out area, the child is required to sit and is not allowed to engage in conversation with anyone. An appropriate length of time for a time-out is usually about ten minutes. A timer is used to signal the end of the time-out, which enables the child to return to the mainstream of the classroom with a minimum of distraction to the others.

If a second time-out is necessary, we send the child home for the day. Parents have been advised in advance not to punish the child if he or she is sent home for loss of control. We suggest to the parents that they keep the child in a quiet room *without access to television* until the regular school dismissal time. Generally, parents are supportive of this practice. Consequently, a child is rarely sent home more than once.

We have found the time-out to be particularly effective in dealing with manipulation, a common behavior problem exhibited by learning disabled children. Recognizing that a child is manipulating someone else takes practice and we continue to learn more each day. Open communicative relationships between the adults involved helps us discover manipulative behavior quickly. Since any given chain of events is usually observed by at least one other teacher on our team, we are usually able to figure out what's going on with a particular child. Sometimes manipulation is hard to detect, especially at the beginning of the year when the children and teachers test each other.

An example of such manipulative testing was Frank's behavior during physical education class. Out of the blue, this angelic-looking child flatly stated, "I won't bounce the ball! You can't make me! My other teacher couldn't make me and you can't either!" We explained again to Frank that one of our class rules was to follow directions and participate. He refused the option of participation and was immediately sent on a time-out. Following each time-out, Frank tested another teacher to see if she would follow through and be consistent. After each time-out, Frank was able to cooperate with that teacher. He learned that there were limits and people who would enforce those limits. He also learned that his manipulative tactics were no longer effective. Much to his surprise, he discovered real personal rewards in group participation.

‖ Socializing Through Class Meetings

We use class meetings to promote attending behaviors and good listening skills. After settling the daily business, we move our chairs into a circle formation for a class meeting where we discuss and try to solve any problems. Active listening techniques, common sense, and personal courtesy are standard operating procedures for talking and listening to each other.

ACTIVE LISTENING

During the class meeting, only one child is allowed to talk at a time, and everyone is expected to listen to what others have to say. We reinforce this behavior by actively listening to only one child at a time. We focus on that child and give only him or her feedback. It can be very difficult, and at times seemingly impossible, *not* to respond to the attention-seeking devices of the other children—calling out of turn, falling over backwards in a chair, poking another child, and so on. We teach the children active listening by asking them to reflect on what another child has said and to tell us how they feel about what was said. We then positively reinforce the children for listening. This reinforcement may take the form of praise or be something tangible.

PROBLEM SOLVING AND SHARING

The topics discussed in the class meeting are chosen from one of the following frameworks: an existing problem, a spontaneous sharing of events and feelings revolving around these events, or a topic introduced by us to initiate discussion and increase language skills.

We discuss existing problems first. Bus problems make up a large part of our discussion in class meetings. Many times the children or the bus driver will bring up a situation that happened on the previous day's bus ride. We might begin the discussion with, "We want to talk about the name-calling on the bus yesterday afternoon between Mike and Bob which ended up with some big threats. What's happening between you two on that?" Sometimes, the children involved may laugh and say, "Oh, that. We forgot all about it and played together yesterday afternoon." If the problem is unresolved or has escalated, then more discussion is in order. A two-person, name-calling incident on the bus on Monday can snowball into a full scale, fist fighting, tray slinging riot in the cafeteria by Tuesday if it is unresolved. Or the classroom may become permeated with tension generated from the situation, which then creates nonattending behavior in the instructional learning groups. A child's attention is easily consumed by thoughts of revenge. By taking the time to resolve a problem when it first comes to our attention, we save immeasurable amounts of time and energy.

The class meeting's relaxed atmosphere allows the students to provide their own solutions to their problems. We list these possible solutions on the blackboard. A discussion follows each solution and a decision is made on the most viable solution to try first. We set up a date when we will all sit down again and discuss how the solution is working. Here's how the system works in practice. Katie and Colin had been calling each other names on the bus for several days. Each child had complained that the other child was always the instigator. During the class meeting, Katie talks about Colin sticking his tongue out at her, and Colin retorts that Katie rolled her eyes at him. They elaborate on what names each one called the other. Some of the other children laugh a little; and, depending on their moods, Katie and Colin might or might not join in. We calmly describe the situation and everyone lists possible solutions, including suggestions from those directly involved. These solutions range from suggestions for physical violence to simply ignoring the person who instigates the situation. We don't list these suggestions for physical violence, since acceptable solutions must be reasonable. We counsel that ignoring minor annoyances is usually the most effective way of initially coping with name-calling. We always listen first to the children's insights and feelings and encourage them to work out their own solutions before offering our own counsel. By working out a reasonable solution to a minor problem, the children learn to work on more complex problems.

BUILDING TRUST AND RESPECT

Presenting class meetings as positive experiences wherein the children feel mutual trust and respect takes time and practice. We work on skills which have been poorly developed. How often are children really listened to and given feedback on what they are saying and are trying to say? How often is television their main source of contact with other humans in this busy, complex society? The students' aggressive behaviors decrease once our class meetings become a part of our daily routine. The children play together more easily. The class meeting brings a sense of belonging and a sense of caring and respect to the classroom. The atmosphere for learning is maximized. The need to act out and to strive for negative attention is eliminated because there are others who respect what the students say and how they feel.

|| The Individual vs. the Group

Reflective listening is a general technique we use in a variety of situations. Though well-known by some teachers, it deserves some explanation here. It is a way of replying to a child, to let him or her know that you are hearing the feelings he or she is having at the moment. The feeling content of what a child has said is restated back to the child, so that it can be focused on. Through reflective listening, the child begins to realize that language is an important method of communicating to others what he or she thinks *and* feels. The child learns that others do care and do value his or her worth.

Examples of trying to hear the children's feelings are demonstrated all day long, beginning as the children jump off the bus in the morning, and everyone tries to talk at the same time. We try to focus on one child at a time, hearing what the child says and acknowledging that we hear. Gary may say "See my new shoes! See my new shoes!" We might reply, "Boy, those shoes are really special, Gary." He may go on to tell us more about getting his shoes and why he is so excited. Or perhaps John has just been tripped by Mike. John screams, "I hate you, you rotten creep!" At this point we may reflect back, "You're really feeling angry with Mike." John may go on expressing his angry feelings. By listening to John and acknowledging his feelings, the anger is often dissipated.

Reflective listening is an indication of our basic conviction about the role of handling feelings as a part of teaching children to handle their own behavior. The interplay between social-emotional problems, problem behavior, and learning problems is, we feel, real and complex. We can't be therapists, but we can work for a recognition of emotions, and often this recognition allows them to dissipate. Confronting problems in a variety of ways is the usual norm—reflective listening is only one technique. This example of an encounter with Gary shows the usual sequence of a typical interaction.

Gary enters the room one morning pushing and shoving Johnny and Susie. Something has disturbed him and he may or may not be able to remain in class. But it's clear that Gary's behavior is a plea for help. On one level, he is asking that limitations on his behavior be redefined. On another level, though, he is asking for recognition that he too is valuable.

Different situations require different approaches. Our strategy is often determined by a kind of informed intuition. In dealing with Gary, we speak to him alone, trying to discover what the problem is. We start out by telling him how we noticed a particular positive behavior. "Gary, you have been doing a super job during the class meetings. We really like what you said yesterday about making friends in your neighborhood." He might then offer a comment that will give us a clue about his current problem. He might say, for example, "I don't like Tony anymore. He pushed me while I was waiting for the bus." We might respond with, "I can see you're really feeling angry with Tony. Let's get Tony and bring him over to talk." A brief chance for Gary to express his feelings may be enough to remedy the problem.

If a solution that satisfies both the child and the teacher cannot be reached, then we would recommend saying something like, "Gary, we understand you're still upset with Tony. But we have our school business to take care of. You'll have to get it together enough to stay with us. Can you do that?" We are there for kids like Gary. We care about all the children, but they also need to know that we will not allow any child to disrupt the rest of the group.

The goal is to maintain a balance between charting behaviors and reaching children on a personal level. Each child is an individual and often has many personal problems, but we also have a responsibility to the total class. It is crucial that the children understand this, understand that there are clear boundaries around their behavior, and that, if the situation gets too troublesome, they will be removed from the group (via time-outs and being sent home). We are frequently amazed how a clear statement of these priorities affects a child's behavior. When it does, we know we are on the way to achieving the right balance between personal wants and the awareness of the needs of others that will eventually allow that child to reenter a regular classroom.

5

‖ Guiding Parental Concern

One of the most difficult jobs a teacher has is to communicate to parents an accurate picture of their child's strengths and weaknesses and how they, as parents, affect their child's educational progress. Indeed, parents have a right to know exactly what kind of progress their child is making in school. But what happens when parents are faced with the fact that their child, who appeared to be bright, happy, and eager enters school and suddenly seems to be a failure at the age of five, six, or seven?

Part of our responsibility is to help parents understand their child who may not be living up to their expectations, dreams, and aspirations. Parental concern is a major factor in helping the learning disabled child reach his or her potential. We help guide this concern through our group meetings and individual conferences by building an atmosphere of informal rapport.

‖ Introducing Parents to the Special Program

Even though the school psychologist has probably already explained the term learning disability, and attempted to alleviate fears that the Special Class for such students is not a class for mentally retarded children, we find that many parents do not accept the diagnosis and placement. Parents often ask if their nonreading, nine-year-old child will catch up to grade level after a year in the Special Class. It is very difficult to say "No, that probably will not happen. At least not that quickly. And, it may never happen." We have to be honest, and to be able to be honest, we have to establish open, direct channels of communication as quickly as possible. The current trend toward increased communication between school and home is vital to a special education program. Most children in regular classes will make it in the world one way or another. But learning disabled children, with their special needs, require the combined efforts of as many understanding adults as possible.

THE ORIENTATION MEETING

Before the group orientation meeting at the beginning of the school year, a letter is sent home urging parents to attend. Even though this meeting is designed as an initial get acquainted time, we begin at that time to allay parental fears, to share our concern, and to lay the groundwork for open communication.

During this meeting we briefly explain our program and present the other support personnel involved with the program—building principal, psychologist, counselor, program director, speech and language therapist, and bus driver. We also survey the group to determine areas of mutual interest for future meetings. This survey contains two sections: one, listing possible children's needs—academic, social skills, self-esteem, and so on; and another, listing parental needs—helping at home with assignments, assisting in carrying out behavior management techniques, and so forth. At the same time, the purpose of the monthly meetings, which is to help parents better understand their child's special problems and to become more effective parents, is clarified. If possible, we encourage any parents who may have participated in former parent programs to talk informally about the benefits of such monthly meetings. We discuss our behavior management system and the good note and conclude the meeting with a decision as to the most convenient day and time for future meetings.

PARENT HANDBOOK

Many parents leave an orientation meeting feeling somewhat overwhelmed by it all. Therefore, we also provide a parent handbook that reiterates the important aspects of our program and communicates useful information. In the pages that follow, we include a breakdown of the different topics covered in the handbook and, where appropriate, actual content that can be adapted to meet the needs of a specific program.

An Introductory Page

The Special Class is a learning situation for children with learning and/or behavior problems who are not functioning up to the learning capabilities demanded in a regular classroom. Your child is fortunate to have an opportunity to participate in this program since the teacher/pupil ratio is two adults to twelve children. We are very lucky to have two fine aides, Ms. _____ and Mr. _____, who have spent many years working with the Special Classes.

Every attempt is made to teach to your child's strengths, while at the same time remediating weaknesses. Often this process is a long struggle, and it is not realistic to expect miracles. Rather, one should appreciate and praise any small gains that are made.

You will be contacted by us many times during the school year. This may be through notes, telephone calls, or conferences and group parent meetings. It is only by working closely together that we can achieve the best possible educational program for your child.

Contacts and Telephone List

Provide a list of all the resource people and personnel the parents might find useful:

- Name of the school (often different from the child's home school), school telephone number, and school hours
- Name of the school secretary and working hours
- Name of the school principal and working hours
- Name of the program psychologist and working hours
- Name of the school counselor and working hours
- Name of the school speech and language therapist and working hours

- School District Office telephone number, name of the Director of Pupil Personnel and his or her working hours
- Transportation Office (bus) telephone number

A Daily Schedule

We include a daily class schedule that lists the time periods for all the different curricula so that parents can visit during a specific lesson if they so desire.

A Summary of Support Services Personnal

This section gives a brief description of the support services personnel and their functions in the program.

You may be contacted from time to time by the program's psychologist, Ms. _____, in order to discuss some retesting information or to talk about your child's progress in the program. In return, you can feel free to contact Ms. _____ if you have any questions or wish to discuss a problem.

Many of our children need speech and language therapy and will be taken out of the classroom for that purpose to work with Mr. _____, our Speech Therapist. You will be notified if your child is receiving speech or language therapy. Suggestions may be sent home on how you can help your child with speech. Also, Mr. _____ is always willing to answer any questions you may have regarding his program.

Ms. _____, our school counselor, is available to discuss any problems you may have. Please refer to her telephone number listed at the beginning of this handbook to call for an appointment.

Last, but by no means least, always know that Mr. _____, our school Principal, is ready with a willing ear. He provides tremendous support to this program and gets to know each one of your children personally.

A Summary of Our Reporting System

In this section, the communication process we use with parents is explained.

In addition to point cards and daily notes, we also utilize telephone calls (occasionally in the evenings, if you work) to help keep you informed about your child's progress in school.

Conferences are held twice a year, usually in October and March. Written reports are provided in January and June. Children in the Special Class do not get letter grades or other report cards as do children in regular classes. In many cases, we find it profitable to have conferences more than the mandated twice yearly. We also hope that you will feel free to contact us any time you think a conference is necessary.

Information on Parent Meetings

This section provides information about monthly parent meetings. We also have found it helpful to hold monthly group parent meetings. These are held in the evenings and we urge both parents to attend. These meetings have been useful in helping parents better understand their child's special problems and needs. In addition, it can be very supportive to meet other parents who are in the same boat. We attempt to present topics that will be of interest to you and always remain open to suggestions for future meetings.

An Explanation of Our Behavior Management System

We define our behavior management system in this section. Behavior is expected to approximate that of children in regular classrooms. Our goal is to accentuate the positive and ignore, as much as possible, the negative. Each child has a point card on which we record points for exhibiting positive student behaviors. (A copy of this card is enclosed.) These cards can be cashed in for small treats or saved in the "bank" for larger prizes.

If a child has had a particularly good day, he or she earns a good note. These notes are quite easy to earn at the beginning of the year. They become more difficult to earn as the year progresses and as we expect higher levels of responsibility. It is very helpful and makes your child feel supported if you give more praise when he or she brings a good note home. Caution—it will be detrimental to our program if you punish your child for not getting a good note. If your child wants to talk about why he or she did not get one, fine. If your child doesn't want to talk about it, please do not push. The next day is usually better!

If a child loses self-control, he or she will be sent on a time-out. This is a period of isolation from other children, usually for about ten minutes, but still under adult supervision. We consider the following to constitute loss of control: hitting other children or the teacher, swearing, disturbing the group so others cannot work, self-destructive tantrums, or refusal to follow directions given by an adult. If it is necessary for a child to have two time-outs in one day, he or she will be sent home for the remainder of the day. The child should stay in his or her room *without television* until regular school dismissal time.

Policy Statement on Mainstreaming

We define our mainstreaming policy as follows:
When we feel that a child is ready socially, academically and emotionally to reenter a regular classroom, every effort is made to find a placement which will meet his or her needs. In the beginning, integration is usually for a short period of time during a nonacademic period, such as physical education or art. If the child can handle that, then the time is increased. Although we realize that it does not always happen, our hope for each child is that he or she will eventually return full time to a regular classroom.

A Summary of Homework Policies

This section explains homework days, materials the child will need to complete homework assignments, and the parents' roles in helping with homework.

Your child will bring home some form of homework every Wednesday. It is to be returned the following day. Every effort will be made to send homework that is self-explanatory. Should your child need help, please give as little direction as possible.
Your child will need such materials as paper, pencils, erasers, crayons, scissors, and paste in order to complete homework assignments. It is also important to establish a regular time to do homework in a quiet, well-lighted area.
Completing and returning homework is part of the process of teaching your child responsibility.
Occasionally a "special" homework assignment will be sent home on a day other than Wednesday. In these cases, it will be accompanied by a letter of explanation.

Cafeteria, Busing, and Field Trip Policies

We define cafeteria, busing, and field trip policies and explain our behavior expectations for each.

Concluding Remarks

Our concluding remarks restate our desire for a cooperative effort in educating the children in the Special Class.

There is really never any conclusion to a child's education—everyone is constantly learning, changing, and growing. We are only here to give your child an extra boost along the way. Together we can help your child reach his or her full potential as a human being.
Thank you for helping us do a better job.

Besides providing a readily available resource for parents, the Parent's Handbook, when it is coupled with the orientation meeting, serves to stimulate participation in the program. When parents understand the Special Program and the need for their roles as active participators, they more readily take an interest in their children's education.

|| Maintaining Parental Involvement

MONTHLY MEETINGS AND PARENTAL AWARENESS

Monthly meetings provide an opportunity to keep parents aware of their child's educational, social, and emotional needs. We offer a diverse monthly meeting program designed to cover topics interesting to the parents.

Naturally, the most effective meetings are those designed around the interests expressed by all those involved. However, sometimes it takes a couple of meetings for people to feel comfortable enough to express their true feelings. So we are prepared with a backlog of available topics. Following are some of those we have used successfully.

Counselor Visitation

We invite a counselor from the local Family Service Agency (or a similar social service agency that deals with youth problems) to explain the services available in the community.

Family Night

The entire family is invited to view "A Walk in Another Pair of Shoes"*, a sound filmstrip available through your regional office of the Association for Neurologically Handicapped Children. The filmstrip explains in simple terms what it is like to have a learning disability. Parents often report that this meeting helped to open discussion within the family and fostered understanding, especially among older siblings.

Rap Sessions

These sessions cover general problems and how to solve them. We are careful not to allow any one situation to turn into an individual conference exclusively between the teacher and one particular parent. Rather we ask the group for solutions on how they handled a similar problem. And yes, we give our opinion too, but we wait until the discussion has progressed to a point where other people will not feel intimidated about speaking further on the subject.

Behavior Modification Discussion

In this discussion (usually introduced by the program psychologist) we define behavior modification and provide guidelines for how parents can utilize this approach for behavior management at home. Employing real examples (using actual cases from within the group, if possible) that show how to choose which behavior to modify, how to present the plan to the child, and how to chart the child's progress and provide appropriate rewards gives parents concrete material with which to work. We don't go deeply into theory, but we are prepared to answer questions from parents who feel behavior modification is a form of bribery. One must feel comfortable with this approach in order to "sell" it to parents.

---

*Barbara Chesler, "A Walk in Another Pair of Shoes." Sacramento, Calif.: California Association for Neurologically Handicapped Children, 1972.

Therapist's Visit

We invite our speech and language therapist to explain her program and provide simple activities parents can use at home. Many learning disabled students have depressed language skills and parents appreciate concrete examples on how they can assist. We found particularly helpful the series of booklets, *Developing Oral Language with Young Children,* by John Murphy and Charles O'Donnel, Educators Publishing Service, 75 Moulton St., Cambridge, Massachusetts 02138.

Activities Night

We sponsor an evening in which we present simple games and activities that can be used to reinforce basic reading and math skills at home.

Show-off Night

Show-off night takes the place of Open House at the end of the year. At this time, all the children perform in some way. The program may include simple dances, exercise routines set to music, or a slide show that demonstrates various aspects of the children's daily school life. In addition, the children present paper flower corsages to their parents and serve punch and cookies (made by the children). The proud smiles we see on the parents' faces makes every second of all the time and effort we devoted to their children worth it.

Some general organizational techniques for group meetings that have proven successful are: a circular seating arrangement so that all the participants can be seen and will feel like they are an integral part of the group; short meetings (an hour is usually sufficient); and a discussion format rather than a lecture situation.

INDIVIDUAL NEEDS AND PARENT CONFERENCES

Although the number of required parent conferences is two per year, we find that four is the average, but there are always some who require even more. In other words, we hold conferences as often as the need arises, not just in October and March. Conferences are necessary in creating a sustained, open line of communication between home and school. A conference is more than just a time to exchange information and develop plans for creating an optimal educational experience. Along with school interactions, it is a time to consider the whole child and his or her relationships to the rest of his environment—home, neighborhood, and community. The fewer stones left unturned, the better the chances of helping the child.

The conference should be held in as relaxed an atmosphere as possible. Parents are often in awe of coming to school. Parents of learning disabled students may be downright fearful, because many of their previous school visits probably originated due to their child being in serious trouble—academically, socially, or both. We meet in the classroom around a table, all sitting in the same size chairs. Remember you can be very intimidating if you project a "tough teacher" image by sitting in a big chair behind a formidable desk. Offer the parents tea or coffee and the option to smoke if they so desire. Then get down to the business at hand—a joint discussion of one child. And remember, this child is *their* child.

Always begin on a positive note. We might share the child's academic progress first then go on to explain the child's reading program and exactly what skills he has gained. Or the opening remarks may just as well deal with the child's progress in social interaction: "Liu said something in our class meeting yesterday that shows that she really cares about other people's feelings." We then go on to relate exactly how it is indicative of positive social growth for the child.

We don't follow any specific topic sequence in the discussion. We do attempt to cover all the curriculum areas as thoroughly as possible and in such a way that the parents will leave with an accurate picture of their child's progress in school. This detailed explanation should include showing them the materials the child uses, samples of the child's work, and demonstrations of the teaching methods that best meet their child's learning style.

Throughout the conference we encourage the parents to contribute, and listening carefully to their responses serves a dual purpose. First, parent responses help paint a more complete picture of the child and his or her world outside the classroom. Second, they may provide an opportunity to make viable suggestions as to how they might handle a particular problematic behavior or situation. The latter is especially important. Let's look at a hypothetical case.

Tim is a child who is abnormally aggressive. While discussing this problem with his parents, they feel comfortable enough to say, "We don't know what to do. Tim is still getting into terrible fights in the neighborhood and a couple of parents have threatened to call the police. We've tried everything and nothing seems to work." Here is an opportunity to offer the parents a possible solution. We might say something like, "You are feeling very concerned about Tim's fighting. We are too. He seems to be having a great deal of difficulty making friends in a positive way. You know, there is a play group run by our local Youth Agency. They have been very successful in working with some of our children in the past." If parents react positively to such suggestions, we give them the number of the agency. We have even gone so far as to make the appointment for the initial visit right then and there.

If the reaction to our suggestion is a negative one, we don't force the issue. Pressure will only alienate the parent from the school. One of the most difficult problems we have had to face is that we cannot change a family's lifestyle, regardless of the tensions it might contain. Until a solution is actively sought by the family with a problem, the best we can do is continue to offer our support. Hopefully, another opportunity will arise that will allow us to offer a constructive suggestion that will be taken.

Yes, parent conferences are physically and mentally draining, and very time consuming. But we use them extensively because they pay off. The traditional report card with As, Bs, and Cs (and in the case of children in the Special Class, a lot of Ds and Fs) does not convey the total picture of our children's progressions or digressions on the path of growth. It's eye-to-eye contact and honest communication between the people who care about that human being that begin to provide a basis for understanding.

BUILDING INFORMAL RAPPORT

In addition to conferences and group meetings, we also employ more informal communication methods. As explained more fully in Chapter 4, the good note communicates to parents their children's progress on a daily basis. Even though the notes are written directly to the child, we encourage parents to share in the positive effects of these notes at home. The presence or absence of a good note lets parents know whether or not their child has had the most constructive day possible in school.

We also use telephone calls to communicate with parents. We don't just call parents during crises—we also call to let parents know about the positive things going on with their child. This is especially effective at the beginning of the year and sets a positive and mutually responsive tone for future contacts. For example, when we first call parents to tell them that their child had a particularly good day at school, the usual response is that this call is the first time a teacher has ever called to say something positive. They are often relieved to hear that someone else can perceive that their child possesses redeeming graces.

We also communicate with the home through a monthly newsletter. The newsletter is written by the children during their language group. The children are the official "reporters," writing articles about what they are studying, their classroom routines, holidays, special projects, field trips, the people in our school, and so on. They also fill in the newsletter with illustrations. We type the newsletter in columns and have the children reproduce them on the duplicating machine. The children are always excited about taking each new edition home to share with their families.

The last informal approach we capitalize on involves chatting with parents we encounter in the community. If by chance we see a parent outside the usual school context, we almost always find a way to spend a few minutes on something positive that happened at school. We may comment on how their child completed a hard math paper that morning. They always go away smiling.

All the techniques described in this chapter are designed to foster an open atmosphere, one that creates a feeling of mutual trust and caring about children. Building such an atmosphere takes a commitment of time and energy on the part of the teacher. But there is no doubt that it's worth it. Parents begin to feel better about their children, and as they do so, the children begin to feel better about themselves! Although the progression to self-management may be slow, as self-esteem builds the children find it easier to take responsibility for their behavior. And it's only a short step from the Special Class to the regular classroom once the children learn to manage their own behaviors.

6

Sending Them On

Mainstreaming children successfully from a Special Class back into the regular classroom involves cooperation in three areas—between the Special Class teacher, the principal, and the regular staff. Each school and each faculty is different and, of course, there is no invariable sequence of steps or stages in the process.

As we discuss in more detail in Chapter 7, the principal plays a large part in creating a receptive atmosphere between the regular classes and the Special Classes. It is true that some principals would still rather not have these classes in their school because they do mean extra work, but efforts to win such principals over is a good investment. It is far easier to mainstream children back into regular classes if the principal is on your side. Hopefully, as awareness grows about what special education is all about, more administrators will gain an understanding of the important roles they play.

Integrating the Special Class with the School

The growing public and academic focus on children with exceptional needs has begun to make all school personnel increasingly aware of Special Class programs and how they function within a school system. We encourage this interest, and avoid representing ourselves as specialists within the school. We participate actively in all regular faculty responsibilities. In doing so, we make ourselves available for discussion about special problems other teachers may be having. We maintain an interest in the behavior of children other than those in our classes; and when we're involved with another child, perhaps on the playground, we are sure to discuss the situation fully with that child's teacher. And we share materials, since we have an extremely wide-ranging supply due to the diverse needs of our class. We also make a point of asking other teachers if we can adapt a particular idea of theirs to the Special Class.

All such overtures build both an awareness and interest in what we do which can later lead to an offer of a placement for a child we are planning to mainstream. We prefer to work for such offers since a placement that is forced is very likely to fail. Nonetheless, it is a delicate matter to negotiate for space in a class for a learning disabled child who is ready (we hope) to try regular work again. Whether the supply of such openings will meet the need at any given time is always a worry.

Successful integration into the school requires the full establishment of our children and ourselves as a part of the school even though we have a largely separate program. Our children, by plan, eat lunch and go to recess with the other classes. The Special Class children are thus mixed in with all of the others and this reduces the problem of the others labeling them and regarding them as different. In addition, the other children in the school see us as "real" teachers, which is important in establishing our children as members of the total school population.

Sharing in yard duty gives us the opportunity to get to other children in the school, which lends us an overall perspective of the total school situation. Children from the other classrooms often drop by after school, sometimes out of curiosity because our classrooms look different, and sometimes because they have had an encounter with us or a child in our room.

Since some of our students do present special problems with control, particularly in large group situations, it is important that other teachers feel that we'll support the discipline of "our" children as long as they're in the school, not just in our room. Both the teachers and our students understand that we are always available to help them work out problems. Often this involves a need for us to repeatedly restate the behavior the child is expected to show, and the consequences for not staying within those limits. For example, Ted is teasing and bickering with another child in the cafeteria. The noontime supervisor tells him to go to another table but he refuses to do so. Ted is known for his temper, so the supervisor comes to us. We go to talk to Ted. We say, "Ted, you were asked to change tables, you refused. Please go and finish eating your lunch in the principal's office. I will come and dismiss you when it is time for class."

Another time a child loses control on the playground. The child fights with the other children to the extent that the noontime supervisor feels that the child needs to be removed from the playground situation. In this case, the supervisor sends for us, and we bring the child inside to cool off and to discuss the problem. We reiterate the consequences for fighting on the playground and see that they are carried out.

Although being this accessible and holding ourselves this responsible is an immense amount of work and a significant energy drain, we see no alternative. We accomplish several things by it, such as communicating to our children that they are to stay within the boundaries set by others as well as ourselves, letting the other teachers know that even when the child is out of our immediate control we will help with his or her behavior, and letting everyone know that our children must also follow the general school rules.

GROUNDWORK FOR CLASSROOM PLACEMENTS

Along with building relationships with the other teachers and working for an atmosphere of general acceptance in the school (more about this in Chapter 7), we take a number of specific steps when we decide that a child is ready both academically and socially for the regular classroom. We begin to prepare the child for the transition, and we seek a placement at an appropriate grade level. As much as possible, we consider the child's and teacher's compatibility. Since the beginnings of mainstreaming take place at our school, we usually have a choice of two classes at any particular grade level. We meet with the regular teacher and discuss the possibility. Our approach is usually something like, "We have a child who is ready to go back to regular class. He is going back to the second grade and we need a place for him to try his wings. Would you be willing to have him for a short period of time each day and see how he does? We could start with a half hour three times a week and later increase the time."

ORIENTING THE REGULAR TEACHER

Our approach always takes into consideration the fact that the regular teacher is now doing something extra. In our work with other teachers, we make it a point to remember what it was like when we were regular classroom teachers. The first few learning disabled children placed with us were difficult because of the added demand to establish a solid structure and firm limits with definite consequences. This is a difficult bill to fill when there are 25 to 30 other children in the class. Whose needs come first—the child's, the teacher's, or the other children's? Having been on the other side we can understand and appreciate the regular teacher's apprehension about assuming those additional responsibilities. And so we prepare the teacher carefully.

We provide a brief synopsis of the child's background, stressing the gains the child has made over his or her special problems. We emphasize that the child needs a "testing ground" before going back to the home school. We tell the teacher that the child should be expected to conform to the regular class policies. We stress that if a child seriously misbehaves, that child will be removed immediately from the regular classroom and returned to ours. We stress that we are there to back up the teacher. We make it clear that the teacher only has to pick up the classroom telephone to call us, and that we expect neither private tutoring nor tolerance of bizarre behavior.

A regular teacher's first experience with mainstreaming is often the most difficult. Once the initial hurdle is overcome, the next time is easier. One teacher expressed her concern and relief after one of our students had been attending class for a month. "I keep waiting for some hideous behavior but he's so good. I can't believe it." (Often, during these integration periods, the children save that hideous behavior for the time they spend in our classroom.)

This work we do to reduce apprehensions and all the back up we offer pays off in the long run. At the time of this writing, we have mainstreamed students with nine out of the twelve teachers in our school. Our staff is remarkably permanent, and consequently it is now much less work to mainstream a child than it used to be. Most of the receiving teachers are well prepared and experienced in the process, and know what to expect.

CHILD COUNSELING

Even though we frequently discuss the process of moving back into a regular classroom in our class meetings, we also counsel the integrating child individually before he actually enters the regular classroom. The first stage of mainstreaming is a frightening time for many of the children. They want to go, and yet they feel that our classroom, and perhaps ours alone, is safe. During the transition period, therefore, we give a lot of support for every positive step they take.

We first approach the child by talking about how much growth he or she has made, how happy we are about this progress, and why we feel that now is the time for the big step. We might say, "Toni, we feel that you are ready to try a regular classroom. We have found a good place for you in Ms. Smith's class. We know you can do it."

The child getting ready to move to the regular classroom may begin showing regressive, acting-out behavior such as teasing, crying, or defiance. He is usually unable to articulate the fact that he both wants and doesn't want to go. He is afraid that he won't make it. Listening and plain talk at this time is crucial. We say, "Yes, it is scary. It is hard. But we know you are ready. You can do it. We believe in you. You don't need us anymore."

Although most of our children are scared about leaving the security of our program, they are usually able and eager to cope with their fear. Often, all that is needed is a little pep talk to send the child happily on his way. On the child's first day, we walk down to the new classroom with the child and jointly meet the teacher. Or we may introduce the child and teacher to each other beforehand.

Our attitude helps set the tone. Our confidence in the children breeds confidence in themselves. Our students draw on their relationship to us, a relationship which often extends over a period of two years. There are usually shared feelings of trust and love. This gives a solid backing to our message that it is time for them to jump back into a regular classroom situation.

Of course, every situation does not go smoothly. An example of this was a boy named Jimmy who was to start attending a fourth grade class for a half hour every day after lunch. As usual, we told him several days in advance that he was going. The moment came for him to go but he refused. "You can send me home or whatever, but I'm not going. The other children will look at me, they'll laugh. I won't go. I won't." We talked fast and encouragingly but to no avail. We knew it was difficult for Jimmy and that he was very insecure. Something in Jimmy's voice told us to drop it for that day. We told him we knew he was feeling scared and that we would try again tomorrow. Then we called his mother and told her about the incident. She agreed to talk to Jimmy that afternoon. Jimmy's mother wanted him to make it too, and she realized what a hard step this was.

The next day we conferred with the regular classroom teacher and she suggested sending two of her students to our room to get to know Jimmy. We decided this would be done best by playing a game. So, the four of us played Monopoly for a half hour. At the end of that time, Jimmy was able to go with them to their class. At the end of his half-hour stint, he came back smiling, but still a little frightened, and presented his special check sheet to us. We gave him thirty points on his point card. The two boys came back the following day at recess to continue the Monopoly game. By the third day, Jimmy was hopping off to the regular class with a wave of his hand.

|| The Process of Mainstreaming

Once the child and the regular teacher are ready to begin integrating, when is the best time to start? Choosing the right time and place for mainstreaming a child into a regular classroom is crucial to successful integration. Both the child and the regular classroom teacher must be ready and willing to take on the pressures that are inherent in making such changes.

We approach a regular classroom teacher at a time when we feel that he or she will be most receptive to accepting a Special Class child in the class. Timing the request is important. If a faculty member is keyed up over writing a new federal funds proposal or the latest revised testing program, the timing is wrong for suggesting the additional pressure of mainstreaming. It is also not advisable to ask a teacher to start taking another child during parent conferences, just before holidays, at the beginning of the year, or anytime that particular teacher is expressing frustration over the daily teaching load. Don't approach a teacher who says "Bobby is driving me up the wall. I've had it."

We begin integration with a short segment of time, such as a half hour, and with an activity that presents a minimum of pressure for the child. If a child enjoys art or music, then it is good to start integration during that activity. Perhaps this activity occurs three times a week, which gives the child and the regular classroom teacher a chance to assess each other and begin to get acquainted under the easiest possible conditions.

Our experiences have been good ones using interest activities as starting points. In all cases, both the child and the teacher have said afterwards, "Gee, that was easy."

The next step might be sending the child to a social studies or science unit taught three times a week for four weeks. Each session might take thirty minutes. If there is any follow-up work, we assure the regular teacher that we will help the child with them. We then give top priority to the completion of that assignment within our class time. This shows the child in a concrete way that we consider the work in "regular" class to be very important. The classroom teacher also feels better about the child and the child's ability to fit into the regular class without too much extra work.

ONGOING COMMUNICATION

Our feedback system is comprised of a behavior checksheet that is completed every day by the child's regular teacher. In this way the regular teacher lets us know how the child is progressing. The child shows the sheet to us when he or she returns to class. Early in the process we ask to see the card as soon as the child returns from the regular class. Later, we say, "We will check your card at the beginning of the morning recess." This procedure then becomes a part of the child's daily routine. Before the time we establish as a check-in time, we sit down with the child, look at the card, and ask how it is going. We discuss any problems or incidents and then give points (which vary in number depending on the time spent in the regular classroom, and the difficulty of the activity the child did while there).

We encourage the regular teacher to keep us informed about the child's behavior in the regular classroom, since it is hard to tell how the child is faring by observing behavior in our room. At this time we often see the child's behavior deteriorate, and, as we've said, it's hard to know whether this acting out is occurring just in our class or in the regular class as well.

We also handle integration problems immediately. For example, let us say that Frank is experiencing difficulty in adjusting to the routines and social patterns in the regular classroom. Frank is mainstreamed on a part-time basis, but he complains that he is constantly teased by his new classmates. After we check with the teacher and ascertain that the teasing is *not* of a serious nature and that Frank has exaggerated the difficulty of the situation, we establish a routine wherein Frank is rewarded for noncomplaining behavior. Every time Frank returns from his regular class, he receives bonus points for not complaining about the other children in it.

INCREASING INTEGRATION TIME

The feedback we get and the support we provide a child lets us know when it is right to increase the child's time in the regular classroom. If all seems to be going well, which means there are no reports from the regular teacher about behavior problems and a decreasing need for support from us, we discuss the other teacher's schedule and identify the next academic area and times which might be best to add to the child's regular room schedule. To determine this, we look for an area in which the child is most

Feedback Checksheet

_____ checksheet on behavior in _____

A.M.	Monday	Tuesday	Wednesday	Thursday	Friday	Comments
Excellent						
Good						
Fair						
Poor						
P.M.						
Excellent						
Good						
Fair						
Poor						

Excellent=50 points   Good=35 points   Fair=10 points   Poor=0 points

A feedback checksheet helps to keep communication lines open among those involved in the mainstreaming process.

confident, but also find out what seems best within the framework of the teacher's schedule. We also check that teacher's perception of the child's ability to fit into a given academic group.

We have found that it takes at least three to four weeks of adjustment time between each time increase. If the child is comfortable with two to two and a half hours in the regular room, then it is likely he or she is ready for a full-time placement, and separation from the Special Class altogether.

Sometimes the child provides the cue as to when to increase time, and the process moves faster. For example, we had integrated Jack for forty-five minutes every morning in a first grade class. Only a few days later he lined up with the first grade class instead of with our class. When we went over to bring him back he asked, "Can I go back to Ms. Smith's class for awhile?" She approved the change and we increased Jack's time to two hours a day. Other children are more blunt and say things like, "I don't like it here anymore," (meaning our class), or "Mr. Kelly's class is better. Why can't I go there?" These comments should not be taken personally. In fact, you should be thrilled by them. It means their wings are getting stronger. Finally the day arrives when the child is ready to fly away for good.

PLANNING FULL-TIME REENTRY

Finding an appropriate placement is essential when the child is ready to go back into the regular classroom on a full-time basis. The full-time experience must be a success and the child's new teacher plays a critical role in producing a positive outcome at this point. Such a teacher must understand the child's needs and provide an environment where those needs can be met.

The larger picture also involves a choice of schools. The first possibility is the child's home school, and in most cases, the child is eager to return to the home school in his or her own neighborhood. Usually with a little groundwork by us and the psychologist, that transition can be smooth and easy.

When the child or the child's parents present strong, negative feelings toward the home school, the second and best possibility is another school within the district. Past experiences with the principal, with teachers, or with other children may present a barrier to the child's getting a fresh start. There may well be a more favorable school within walking distance or within the radius of a short bus ride on public transportation.

The third possibility is placement in the same school the Special Classes occupy. This is a perfectly workable alternative when the child either appears to need the additional support of remaining at the school where his first successes have been accomplished, or needs to be near us. In this case the parents must provide transportation to and from school for the child.

When the child returns to a regular classroom in another school it is not easy for us to maintain contact. Although some families and children return to visit us, this is the exception after the first two or three months of the placement. We know that the child is not left completely alone, as there is a learning disability group (LDG) specialist available in the other school. Through these colleagues we sometimes hear details of the child's progress. But meantime there is the whole cycle to begin all over again with a new placement, and the inevitable demands of the ongoing group.

7

Teamwork, Support, and Survival

Team teaching is, we feel, a major element in our success and in our continued commitment to our work. In this chapter we describe some of its benefits, and we hope that other teachers will become inspired to begin work on similar professional relationships. The reader should keep in mind that we have been working on this approach for six years now and that everything described here certainly wasn't realized in the first year. However, we began with no particularly unusual resources and without access to specially adapted classrooms. No one told us to become a team, and team teaching is not recommended in California's Educationally Handicapped program descriptions. Yet, neither is it prohibited or discouraged.

Teaming Up

Teaming up has given us a profoundly valuable gift—mutual support. Teaching can be a lonely profession when one class of children is assigned to one teacher, particularly if that class is "special" and regarded as somewhat different from the regular school population. The one-to-all situation all too often leads to a feeling of isolation, stagnation, and eventual burnout. Team teaching, we are convinced, helps to alleviate these liabilities, and increases the effectiveness of the program. We accomplish more in less time, present fuller and more objective evaluations, and keep our energy and interest at high levels.

High teacher interest and energy is particularly vital to the success of a Special Class program. The teacher must continually recharge the children's desire to learn while continually working against the weights of disabilities and previous failures. We keep our interest level high by dividing teaching responsibilities according to our individual skills and interests—we both don't try to do everything. For example, although we both teach reading, we do not attempt to mirror each other's teaching approaches. In our work with children who have had severe difficulties learning to read, we have both developed different types of materials and techniques to work with the various learning modalities. By pooling our resources and strengths, we provide all the essential elements but also don't feel overburdened. By team teaching, we are able to like what we are doing, and how we are doing it.

Team teaching, therefore, produces a more creative curriculum and a more supportive atmosphere for our students. By teaming, we can offer a variety of activities and programs not possible in the one teacher classroom. Class meetings, film viewings, discussions, and field trips offer opportunitites for our students to work and play in groups and to prepare for integration into the regular classroom. One of us can provide more individual attention when a child needs that one-to-one contact, while the other handles direction and guidance for the rest. And we can shift roles to accommodate such needs very quickly.

Although the person in charge of a unit has the responsibility for planning, this should not rule out discussing needs for particular materials with the other teacher. We are all scavengers from necessity and for fun, and quite often one person can more quickly obtain some material than another. The value of collectively hunting for needed materials cannot be overemphasized. We have found that between the four of us, for example, we can usually come up with enough ice cream freezers, woks, and giant mixing bowls to cook every type of concoction we desire.

We don't individually attempt to cover all aspects of each subject area. In language arts, one of us is more successful in teaching the group to write a short story about an experience while the other finds teaching poetry writing easier and more productive. In math, one of us has more skill working with preconceptual or concrete level programs while the other works better with the operational stages of a program.

The major teaching responsibilities for other curriculum units shift back and forth between us depending upon the particular situation, individual skills, and our interests. Taking charge of cooking projects, physical education activities, social studies units, and field trips is usually fun for one of us while science, art, and music activities flow naturally from the other. Sometimes we do separate the children into smaller groups, each of us handling the actual teaching of the unit or lesson. But one teacher is still responsible for the planning and organization of that unit. In general, small groups work better for us in art and science while music, physical education, and social studies work yields better results in larger group settings.

Another benefit of team teaching is the extra guidance provided for each child. Having more than one adult with whom to identify increases the child's chances of communicating his or her needs. Each child communicates differently at different times and in different situations. For teachers working in a team such as ours, this shift in patterns presents little or no problem. At any given time, there are two, three, or four sets of adult antennae up to catch what a child is trying to express—and chances are that one of them will be tuned in correctly.

We can use Jimmy's story to illustrate the benefit of having these extra sensitivities available. Jimmy was having difficulty moving back into a regular classroom. He expressed negative feelings about the teacher and the children in that classroom via such comments as "I don't want to go there. Billy always teases me and I get in trouble." These rather blatant clues that all was not going smoothly conflicted with his homeroom teacher's opinion and the opinion of his regular classroom teacher. They were convinced that the placement was correct. Jimmy was ready academically. Socially, he had problems, but his home- room teacher felt that he was ready to meet them. When she tried to talk to Jimmy, though, she encountered a wall of defensiveness, failing to get through it even after trying a number of times to do so. Then one of our aides (more about our aides below) quietly took Jimmy aside. She got him to agree that he was to tell her one positive thing that happened to him each day in that classroom. Their private sharing time was to take place right after Jimmy returned from his hour in the regular class. Her insight and rapport with him proved to be the key, and the problem dissipated. Within days Jimmy had stopped complaining, and he went to the regular class with a fair amount of confidence.

The input of several adults who work directly with the child is invaluable when evaluating the child's progress on a daily basis, in informal quarterly conferences, and in written reports. A child always has some areas that are stronger than others, and if the child has the opportunity to be observed with the greatest possible objectivity, the chances for success increase. If one teacher is teaching all the subject areas, both teacher and student may let one unfavorable time together prejudice their overall view of one another. If they can take a break from one another and go on to other people and experiences, then each day brings new perspectives and a fresh start.

When we all sit down and evaluate the children, each teacher brings up the strengths she has seen and the key areas on which individual children are working. A casual observation by one teacher often triggers a chain of observations about that child by other teachers. One teacher may mention how Sally made an offhand remark during math about her mother being in the hospital. Perhaps she had been acting up with another teacher. An objective discussion about Sally's home situation and how it has affected her classroom behavior will ensue, thereby allowing us to understand her in a new light. Later, a little checking and talking with Sally will help her cope with her difficulty a little better. Usually, after this kind of approach to acting-out behavior, the child is able to rechannel herself back into the learning situation.

INSTRUCTIONAL AIDES AS TEAM MEMBERS

Although we are the core of the team effort in the classroom, we expand our conception of the team to include our

instructional aides, particularly as they take on more responsibilities. Our aides soon come to function at the same
professional level. In fact, we refer to them as "teachers" since
they regularly assume responsibilities that are outside their job
description. We are incredibly fortunate to have two aides who
have 11 years of experience working with learning disabled
children. But even with this experience, our aides seek to learn
more all the time and to become more involved in the classroom
action. We continually point out that we're all there for the
same purpose.

Our aides are constantly expanding their roles as they take
the initiative for assuming more responsibility and building new
skills. With a few ideas and materials from us, our aides have
built top-notch individual programs in math and language arts.
They have also designed a motor development program, and
have attended classes and workshops on dance, yoga, and
movement exploration, incorporating ideas from each of these
into their work.

Even though they have an intrinsic motivation to do the best
possible job, they too need to be recognized and appreciated for
all their extra work. Since their monetary compensation is
slight (clerical level salaries) compared with their services, we
make a point to gain recognition for them in as many ways as we
can. We have discussed their services with the school principal,
written letters to the personnel department that explicitly
stated the extent of their services, and frequently told them
how much we appreciated them. Of course, none of this pays
them their due monetarily, but these outward expressions of
appreciation do let our aides know that we feel gratitude for
their gift of dedication to the children.

THE CONDITIONS OF TEAMWORK

The benefits we've outlined can't be realized, of course,
unless the team members have worked out ways of cooperating
to a high degree. The ideal team teaching combination produces
a cooperation among individuals so complete that personal
energy, ideas, and feelings can be given without risk. Each team
member understands that what is being offered is involvement

on a personal level and is willing to share freely—mentally, emotionally, and physically—in the educational process.

Effective team teaching is a total sharing of ideas on curriculum, behavior management, and teaching approaches. Such cooperation does not develop instantly or easily, we have found. Mutual respect for individual strengths and teaching styles must exist as the basis for open communication.

Children immediately sense whether this situation exists, and whether all members of the team are working together. At the beginning of each year, the students run a brief battery of tests primarily to check our cohesion as a working group. This exercise may be as minor as "Miss X told me I didn't have to do that paper now," (something which in the complexity of our classroom could be true) and if Miss Y can't check with Miss X quickly and openly, the students will expand on this "But *she* said" game.

More importantly, however, our classroom team has to be and usually is together on the definition of standards for acceptable behavior. If a particular behavior is unacceptable in one group, then it is unacceptable in the others. Consistency in maintaining these standards requires constant communication among all of us because so many individual needs and objectives are being met. Some behavior is absolutely forbidden all year, but other standards need to be adjusted and monitored continually. A comprehensive and inflexible code of conduct doesn't do the job.

There can be disagreement between the adults involved but we make sure it never becomes a win or lose situation. The awesome power of humiliation, intentional or not, must be held in check. Each team member must understand the fragility of what is being sought by the students and the teachers— involvement of one's total self in the learning process.

In order for us to live in this highly vulnerable state, we've found it essential to nurture a sense of humor. Learning does not proceed like clockwork, and laughter recharges human batteries. When a lesson or an hour becomes unmanageable because the carpenter is hammering away replacing the window, the sixth grade band is rehearsing next door, the baby bird with a hurt wing discovered at recess is now in the classroom, or Billy just split his pants down the back, a little laughter and shifting of gears saves more than just the day. The alternatives, taking oneself and one's prior plans absolutely seriously, leads to nervous breakdowns and is just plain *boring* as well.

A cautionary note, though. We are talking about a laughter that is quiet and shared with the children. We have found that most learning disabled children (and most young children in general) have a quite different sensitivity to humor than adults do, and our adult humor may be badly misinterpreted by them.

|| Support Personnel

A Special Class program is as strong as the support it receives in the classroom, in the school, and in the community. We work closely with educational specialists, concerned school personnel, and groups outside the school in a team effort to create a total education for our children—academic, social, and emotional.

Our own personal and professional relationships based on years of experience working together comprises the core of this team effort. We show other people involved with the children how we provide support so that the whole environment becomes as supportive as it can be. We jointly make detailed decisions and plans about daily routines, program plans, and communications with parents and other school and district staff. In short, we carry the final responsibility for the implementation of the child's education.

From us, the team's energies spread out like ripples in water where a pebble has been dropped—each ripple, or person who touches the child, holds potential significance for the child's development and education. We call upon the district psychologist, the school counselor, and the speech and language therapist for guidance and advice. We involve our school principal in our program activities. We confer with the local social service agency that links our program to the community, and more.

THE PRINCIPAL

A Special Class's effectiveness relies heavily on the principal's special support. We have heard many stories about special education classes being relegated to the back forty and viewed only as a necessary evil. If the principal ignores a Special Class, a tremendous support system is missing. If the class is in conflict with the principal, it's an impossible situation. But, if the principal is a warm, empathic, effective human being who wants your program in the building, the chances for a successful program are increased.

A supportive principal can serve as a liaison with the district office administration when problems arise. Problems requiring the principal's assistance might include conflicts about a child's placement in the program, bus schedule conflicts, granting leaves, or the hiring of substitutes. Standard operating procedure requires that such problems be managed at the building level first, but the next step is to ask the district office for assistance. A principal's request will enhance the chances for a quick resolution.

A person in this administrative position can also solve many routine matters such as obtaining materials and furniture. The principal will know about surplus supplies or those which can be obtained through an exchange. For example, for two years we asked for junior executive desks which we felt would be far superior to the lift-top variety we had. We made written and verbal requests to our principal. Mysteriously, he produced some that were in storage in another building.

We are fortunate to work with a principal who supports our program both personally and professionally. Not only does he laugh at our jokes, represent us well to the district office, and produce needed supplies, but he also:

- Reinforces the children's positive behavior. At the end of the day, the children visit our principal with their good notes. He writes his own message on the note, giving it added power at home.

- Gets to know our children personally. Our principal attends class meetings, participates at class parties, and visits our class often. He constantly looks for individual growth. He *makes* the time for our students.

- Gets to know the children's parents. Our principal attends our evening parent meetings and participates without dominating. He also attends other family functions we hold such as Open House. His interest helps others see the school as a positive place and also builds a foundation for open communication with parents. Because he establishes this *before* a crisis occurs, he makes it far easier to handle crises.

- Gives his help in difficult situations when we ask for it. If we are having a conference with a parent about a problem we invite him and he finds ways to deliver a strong and clear message to a parent. But he also knows how to stay out of the discussion until his authority is needed.

- Succinctly and firmly draws the lines of acceptable behavior when a child loses control. The children know that the principal has authority but that he uses it sparingly. Each necessary exercise, therefore, carries more impact.

- Sets the tone for acceptance of the Special Class by the total staff. Our principal sees us as important, full members of the faculty. He addresses our problems in private and at staff meetings. He considers our needs along with the rest of the staff.

We have found teaching Special Classes to be emotionally and physically draining. If our building principal was not so supportive, the difficulty of our job would increase geometrically. We would have little energy left for building our program and serving as advocates for the children.

THE PSYCHOLOGIST

The psychologist plays a key role in the child's adjustment to the Special Class program. She is responsible for the initial testing and referral process while the child is in a regular class or during transfer from another program or district. The psychologist makes the recommendation for placement in the Special Class, explains the program to the child's parents, and lays the groundwork with the child. If this groundwork is thorough, and includes observations of the class by the child and the parents, then the child will more readily make a full adjustment to the Special Class program.

Once the child is placed in our class, the psychologist is a resource for full implementation of the program with an ongoing assessment of the child's progress. When appropriate, the psychologist makes recommendations for placement in an alternative program.

THE SPEECH AND LANGUAGE THERAPIST

The speech and language therapist plays a vital role in working with Special Class children, their teacher, and their parents. Our therapist's expertise in language development, processing, and articulation goes far beyond our knowledge. We often work with the therapist even when a child's problems seem to have no connection with speech and language.

Joel's case was a perfect example of the resourcefulness of our therapist. We were convinced Joel was just weak on attending behavior, but although we worked on that with him, Joel continued to have a problem following directions. We conferred with the speech and language therapist, and she subsequently administered the Illinois Test of Psycholinguistic Abilities. She said that Joel's problem was not one of attention, but that his concept understanding and auditory processing were not well developed. The therapist explained that Joel should be given simple, one-at-a-time directions. We followed her advice, and found Joel's attending abilities rapidly improved.

The therapist also helps us in working with parents. Since language problems are prevalent among learning disabled children, we ask our speech and language therapist to give a parent workshop at one of our monthly meetings. She has a simple list of things parents can provide at home, and she explains it so that parents actually use the techniques.

THE SCHOOL COUNSELOR

The school counselor is often tremendously valuable to us. Over the years, our counselor has helped us with behavior management and provided fresh insights into working more effectively with parents. She has also served as coordinator with outside social service agencies. Our counselor, with whom we have worked so successfully for many years, continues to encourage us and support our interests in working with learning disabled children. She listens to our frustrations and helps us remember that we *can't* change everything about a child's life that we would sometimes like to!

THE LOCAL SOCIAL SERVICE AGENCY

In our community, the Youth Service Bureau, (which is supported by city, county, and local school district funds) is an invaluable resource for helping to solve child-parent conflicts. We may become aware of such conflicts during a parent conference, since we don't discourage parents from bringing up problems they are having with their child. When we hear about children lying, stealing, or exhibiting other behaviors that indicate emotional problems, we refer the family to the Youth Service Bureau for counseling.

Our bureau has a staff of three counselors who work on a short-term basis with children who have difficulty with their families or with the outside world. These counselors work closely with the schools and with the juvenile section of the police department. Before a counselor begins working with a child, he or she often comes to the school and observes the child. The counselor then confers with the child and the parents both individually and together.

We ask a representative from our local social service agency to speak at one of our parent meetings on the ways in which the agency has helped families with problems. These informal down-to-earth discussions have encouraged many families to use the Youth Service Bureau; recently, one-third of our children's families received assistance from this agency. In most of those cases we could see the benefits within a short time.

ADDITIONAL SUPPORT PERSONNEL

The school secretary, noontime supervisors, the custodian, and all the others who work in the school have the potential for becoming positively involved with our students. We do not think that support for growth and change or for a sense of self-worth comes only from professionals. It is the child who decides how important any relationship is at a particular time. The child reaches out and allows himself or herself to be touched by another person, making that person an important part of his or her life. We actively cultivate relationships with school personnel so as to gain acceptance for our children, as we never know where or when a child might get something he or she needs from outside the classroom.

For example, one year when the school building was being painted, one of our students, Donny, was put on a bench for fighting on the playground. The painters were working nearby, and one of them began to talk to him. From that small incident, a relationship blossomed. The painter was a local Little League coach and was eager to help us when he became aware, through Donny, of our needs. While he was on the painting job he taught baseball skills to our children at recess and provided baseball jerseys that became highly valued prizes for good behavior. The important point here is that the children, and especially Donny, felt that someone was genuinely interested in them, someone who didn't *have* to be.

We have found it important to communicate our values about this kind of relationship to everyone who may provide it. This is the general theme we play to everyone around us, painter to school secretary, in varying words but always with the same essence: Everyone involved with the child must be in close, honest communication with each other, and have the child's development as a common goal, if the child's growth is to be best served. The child may at times not relate to his teachers, so we always encourage others to help. Any member of the classroom team or any of the people outside the classroom may be sought out by a child. The seeking out and sharing are messages of respect, and any person for whom the child shows respect has an edge in helping the child at that particular time.

|| Survival Tips

WHAT TO EXPECT

The kind of day that can threaten one's sanity in a Special Class situation is outlined below. The report is factual and accurate down to the last letter (and practically to the exact minute).

7:05 Receive telephone call from your aide saying she is sick and won't be in today. Reassure her that everything will be fine.

7:07 Same aide calls again and says she hates to tell you but she just received a call from the other aide, and she is sick also.

7:08 Continue to reassure.

7:10 Finish getting dressed. Throw some bread in the toaster. Grab a cup of coffee.

7:15 Make lunches, drink coffee, and quiz son for spelling test.

7:30 Begin breakfast for unexpected out-of-town guests who arrived the night before.

7:50 Put out cat and dog. Insist son wear hat to school since storm is raging outside.

7:55 Settle who will have the car with daughter. She drives you to school.

8:00 Sign in at school. Secretary tells you that district office can only get one substitute aide.

8:05 Mr. and Mrs. Smith arrive for morning conference.

8:35 Organize some of materials that aide usually handles.

8:45 Call district office to find out if they have found a substitute teacher for second aide. Answer is no. You insist they continue to try. They say they'll get back to you before 9:00 a.m.

8:50 One subsitute teacher arrives to take the aide's place. Show her where materials are for math groups she'll be teaching.

8:55 Run to get a cup of tea. Get message from principal that district office has contacted him about Special Class teachers upsetting the clerk who gets substitutes. Tea on table gets cold.

8:57 Call boss at district office. Explain content of your call to "substitute-getting" clerk. Yes, he understands. No, no, they cannot get a second sub.

9:00 First bus arrives while you're still on phone to district office. Your team teacher takes kids to class.

9:05 Another child arrives by car. Bus missed him.

9:07 Run down hall to see if second bus is here.

9:10 Another child arrives by car.

9:12 Run down hall to see if second bus is here.

9:15 Mother arrives with child in tow—child who is spending a first-time half-day visitation as possible Special Class student. Reassure mother. Introduce child to some kids in the class.

9:18 Quick conference with team teacher. Reorganize groups since short one teacher.

9:20 Second bus arrives fifteen minutes late due to rain flooding the highway.

9:22 Begin class meeting!

Have now been out of bed for two hours and twenty minutes.

9:23–5:14

Synopsis of rest of day:

- One child brings note from mother stating that he was sick to the stomach that morning and she didn't know if he would be able to stay in school. Prepare child for fast exit from classroom.
- Rainy day recess and you have the duty.
- One child loses lunch ticket.
- Afternoon bus is late and you have to stand outside in gale force winds with twenty-one kids waiting in line for ten minutes. Bus leaves parking lot at 2:25 p.m.
- Parent conferences between 2:30 and 4:30. One crisis situation and two regulars.
- Put together and organize homework, tasks usually completed by aides.

5:15 Leave for home to cook dinner for guests who have decided to spend another night.

This particular day was reconstructed by Sylvia, who on the evening in question began to wonder just what had really happened to make her feel as if she might never see another day of teaching. She wrote down these events, reconstructed the times, and shared the document with the rest of us the next day.

We were able to laugh at the complexity of the day's demands and the many moments that had required split-second changes in plans or spontaneous action.

All of us have used this strategy of writing down a particular day's demands on occasion, but the teaching team relies most constantly on an attitude and a commitment to get us through days like this and to keep our spirits up for succeeding days which may be just as demanding.

THE CLEAN SLATE ATTITUDE

During our first year of teaching the Special Class, the day came when we decided to put all the children together in the same room at the same time. We had the clever idea we would gather the children around a big work table so they could decorate a large cardboard box to hold our recess equipment, feeling the activity would foster a feeling of class togetherness. Instead, what happened was a classic example of contagion: a rapidly spreading, usually corrupting, influence that begins with one and quickly spreads to everyone. In this case, it began with one large jar of brown paint and Arthur's preoccupation with various aspects of elimination, and soon became a highly descriptive discussion on bathroom talk and bodily functions. We tried to change the subject, but to no avail. So we just stood back and let the kids grovel in it, thinking what a great observation this would make for some college class. Fortunately, the bus arrived before the seminar developed into an actual demonstration.

After this experience we resolved that no matter how many times contagion started rolling, we would stick to our *clean slate attitude.* Many years ago a wise teacher, who had more experience than we did, told us that one of the most important things a teacher should remember was that no matter what happened on a particular day, the next day was a new one and was to be started absolutely fresh. This meant that no matter how infuriating a child's behavior was on Tuesday, you were to put the old memories aside and give him the benefit of the doubt on Wednesday morning. She called it her clean slate theory, and to practice it guaranteed you would not retire directly from teaching to the local sanatorium.

UNWINDING AT THE END OF THE DAY

A part of our daily routine involves the entire classroom team sitting down at the end of the school day to review the day's events. Not only does talking about frustrations relieve tensions, but the group itself becomes a sounding board for any unresolved problems and for making future plans. Nothing takes the sting out of what we consider a personal affront to our dignity by a child better than a humorous interpretation from our coworkers. We feel it is dangerous to our own sense of balance to get so involved in teaching that we miss the small episodes that make teaching so interesting and rewarding. To be able to laugh at and accept our own mistakes is all part of the growing process. And if we are growing, it helps the children grow as well.

After an unwinding period, we generally find ourselves ready to buckle down for the next day's plans. Getting all the silly stuff out of the way clears the air for the serious business of evaluating where the children have gone on that particular day and planning for the direction to be taken the next day.

Perhaps more than any other element of our work, this commitment to mutually lighten, place in perspective, reinforce, and finally begin again makes the overall task feasible year after year. It shares responsibilities broadly that otherwise might become a major burden if held alone, and it is a reinforcement of the qualities that a Special Class teacher *wants* to master:

The Special Class Teacher

S sincere	C caring	T tenacious
P persistent	L lively	E effective
E energetic	A accepting	A active
C creative	S sociable	C competent
I in-tune	S searching	H hardy
A available		E enterprising
L loving		R resourceful

In the hope that all our colleagues working with learning disabled children strive for these qualities as we do, and in the hope that our description of our program helps a little toward that objective, we conclude our discussion of our *Room to Grow*.

Afterword: Advocacy for the Learning Disabled

We have come to realize that we have a responsibility to the children we teach, and to other learning disabled children, that extends beyond the classroom. It is in their interest if we work to increase awareness of learning disabilities, and prod those who are aware and involved to find ways of serving families and children better than they do now.

Awareness is the first priority with most people we meet and talk to, because learning disabilities are invisible. These children look like other children. Most people assume they will need no special help, that they will follow a normal course through school, and become functioning, self-supporting adults. Unfortunately, this is not the case. The disabilities become obvious to teachers (although still not to some others) as soon as the children are exposed to the rigors of learning to read and write. And even with special education programs many learning disabled children will carry their disabilities throughout life. The degree of compensation and the level of coping skills an individual achieves will vary, but a certain percentage of students will require special programming or assistance all the way through college if they are to reach their potential. Many of those who might be able to provide some of that assistance are not likely to know of the still invisible disability unless they know how to look for it.

For those people who are already mandated or committed to serving the learning disabled, the problem is not one of a lack of awareness. The real problem is bureaucratic fragmentation and unwillingness to deal cooperatively with others. We have gone farther than most teachers in our contacts with social service agencies, physicians, and the like, and often have experienced frustration. In the hopes that other teachers, as well as any doctors, social service workers, and others who may read this can be of some small help in these areas, we describe some of our experiences.

|| Bureaucratic Fragmentation

It is sometimes necessary (or highly desirable) to have all the people involved with a child's problems together at the same place and the same time, for a full case conference—and it also seems virtually impossible to do so. It seems to be a major undertaking to get all the school district people involved with a child into such a conference, to say nothing of a doctor, a psychologist, and a social worker.

Consequently, we often find ourselves serving as a communications channel between different parties, although this is an uncomfortable position and an unassigned one. At one conference we might meet with the child's parents and an outside (private) psychologist. Another time, we may be involved in a crisis meeting with the principal and a social worker. And at yet another, we may meet with the school's psychologist and speech therapist, and the principal. But we are not in a good position to convey opinions or recommendations from one professional to another.

We think one solution is to give a district psychologist the role of bringing together all involved persons. In the school hierarchy, the psychologist has more status with the outside world than a teacher, and therefore has a better chance to serve as coordinator between various professionals. However, we haven't had a lot of success in promoting this idea so far, largely due to the heavy demands on our district's psychologists.

SOCIAL SERVICE AGENCIES

County social service agencies are always overbooked and understaffed, but red tape and conflicting regulations seem to compound this situation. We remember one boy, whom we'll call Todd, whose case exemplifies the damage that can be done when no one person systematically follows a case, or when some regulation stops action at a crucial point.

Todd's unmanageable behavior and low academic achievement brought him to our class, where his academic skills quickly improved. While he was in our class, his behavior was manageable, but his behavior in the lunchroom and during recesses was not. We looked into Todd's personal life to discover keys to his behavior at school, and found that Todd's family life was extremely disruptive. This was preventing him from attending school some days and causing him to be late when he did attend. We also learned that he often went without meals, wandered around the city late at night, and was, reportedly, drinking.

During the two years that Todd spent in our class, we had numerous conferences with members of Todd's family. Our primary goal was to get them to provide adequate supervision and care for Todd; we said this meant regular meals, providing Todd a quiet place to sleep, and seeing that he was home and in bed on school nights by 9:00. We didn't get anywhere.

The county social service agencies had been involved in many ways with the family, and we talked with several workers who were successively assigned to the case. The reshuffling of the case from person to person and department to department used up a lot of time and energy during those two years, and finding the right person to talk to was a challenge. When we finally did contact that magical person, we were repeatedly informed that until Todd did something that caused him to be arrested, they would only *talk* to the family when they had a chance. (They agreed to talk with *us* only after many phone calls.) We were told that under new regulations, every effort was being made to keep the child in the home. In the spring, Todd was picked up several times by the police for shoplifting, and finally sent to a relative's home for a month.

We had sent Todd on from our program prior to that, because his academic skills had improved dramatically. In the fall he went back into a regular class, but he was unable to cope. He was suspended within the first month of school. By the end of the first semester, the school district and Todd's mother agreed to place him in a residential school, but Todd never made it there. Although his mother and the district had made the decision, the social agency had to handle the placement. That process was drawn out from December to June. Before June, the mother moved to another school district, seeking help, and that's when we lost track of Todd. The case typifies the waste of effort (ours included) that resulted from fragmented procedures in the agency. If there had been one worker consistently pushing for the placement when it was needed, we felt, it would have been realized in a few weeks. Had regulations permitted earlier action, Todd might even have made a successful transition into a regular class.

Our efforts with our local social service agency, the purpose of which is to meet immediate needs, have been more successful. We frequently refer our students and families to them for short term counseling, and the agency people follow up with case conferences and phone calls. The proximity of the agency and its small size contribute to its efficiency. They are generally knowledgeable about our program and the schools in general, and they appreciate the fact that we're both interested in a child's total situation and willing to work with them to improve it.

THE ROLE OF DOCTORS

We have frequently been frustrated by doctors' lack of interest in learning disabilities. This concerns us because in the case of young children, a doctor is often in the best position to discern an emerging problem or to ask questions about the family and child if something seems wrong. One step we have thought of taking is to duplicate and share the following items from Helen Gofman's "Index of Suspicion," with any doctor who will listen. We explain that these items are possible indicators of the existence of a learning disability that might be quietly checked out if a parent mentions any one, or if the child is judged distractible or very easily frustrated.

- Child is male—many more males than females are affected.
- Family history of learning disabilities or educational difficulties.
- Lag in development, judged by stages of speech development and large and small motor coordination.
- Illnesses or accidents involving central nervous system.
- Hyperkinetic syndrome—distractibility, short attention span, emotional liability, low frustration tolerance, poor impulse control.
- Any indication of seizures—"staring" behavior, perceived loss of contact with the child momentarily, or lapses in muscle control.
- Cultural factors—different language or behavior standards from the mainstream culture.
- Dysfunctional home environment—marital stress, very unequal parenting, and similar factors.*

It has been hard to convince physicians, even pediatricians or psychiatrists, that they could be making a major contribution to a family's welfare by spotting a potentially disabled child. And although we've provided many written comments on children going for physicals, and indicated our willingness to confer directly with the doctor, we have found only a handful of these professionals who have asked for our observations.

Learning Disabilities and Juvenile Delinquency

Numerous sources we've consulted concur that difficulties in school (many initially caused by learning disabilities) correlate with a tendency toward juvenile delinquency and later

---

*Helen Gofman, "The Physician's Role in Early Diagnosis and Management of Learning Disabilities," Learning Disabilities—Introduction to Educational and Medical Management (Springfield, Illinois: Charles C. Thomas Publishing, 1969), pp. 120-126.

antisocial behavior. This makes our work of concern to not only the individual and his or her family, but to society at large. It is clear that control by incarceration after real delinquency has begun isn't successful—the recidivism rate is about 85%.

We are not saying that all learning disabled children will become delinquents, just as we are not saying that all delinquents are learning disabled. However, the correlation between the two is too startling to ignore and convinces us that it is vital to keep on fighting for the recognition of learning disabilities as a problem which has consequences beyond the home and school.

The answer seems to us to be early diagnosis and prescription, followed by successful therapy managed by families, teachers, and pediatricians. We therefore encourage the earliest possible recognition of learning disabilities in our district. We are careful not to let referrals carry over from year to year and we talk to other teachers about the importance of early diagnosis and extra help for certain children. As noted, we work with parents to help them learn the seriousness of acting-out behavior, and ways of bringing it under control.

We are in a good position to detect early signs of learning disabilities when the child first enters school and before maladjusted behavior becomes fixed. But there is a long way to go before we achieve the kind of cooperation and communication we would like between parents, physicians, social workers, and others. If we can successfully foster a concentrated kind of cooperation in these early years, we see a great hope that all of these children will reach their maximum potential, and hopefully avoid the strain that an older and chronically frustrated learning disabled child often puts on the family, the neighborhood, and perhaps eventually on the society at large.

‖Appendix

Basic Sight Words Test

Level II Words

they		
did	that	going
come	who	like
no	had	saw
an	long	yes
around	three	this
ten	was	just
soon	got	if
from	its	some
say	fly	then
under	but	as
stop	before	walk
make	out	his
help	your	ride
sleep	call	here
pretty	cold	will
round	them	when
funny	am	white
of	put	take

Level III Words

or	ran	work
with	there	about
after	what	ask
sing	must	five
myself	over	cut
let	again	new
well	have	how
keep	drink	sit
made	went	upon
give	once	together
us	tell	ate
where	many	warm
laugh	live	now
came	buy	very
hold	would	not
open	light	their
pull	may	goes
small	found	read
were	best	because
grow	fast	off
draw	bring	got
always	much	does
show	any	try
kind	wish	carry
know	only	pick
don't	gave	every
has	seven	right
why	please	clean
been	never	those
write	first	these
both	shall	own
hurt	eight	wash
full	use	done
start	get	find
could	fall	think
far	which	our
want	thank	better

Advanced Basic Sight Words Equivalent to Fourth Grade Words

more	than	other
such	even	most
also	through	years
should	each	people
Mr.	state	world
still	between	life
being	same	another
white	last	might
great	year	since
against	used	states
himself	few	during
without	place	American
however	Mrs.	thought
part	general	high
left	united	number
course	war	until
something	fact	though
less	public	almost
enough	took	yet
government	system	set
told	nothing	end
called	didn't	eyes
asked	later	knew

Decoding Skills Test (Examiner's Copy)

Student's Name _____

Age _____

Examiner _____

Fall Date _____

Spring Date _____

Directions: Give child the student copy of test (typed in primary type). Have the child read across each row for first 4 sections. Have the child read down each column for last 2 sections.

Mastery: Circle each correct response. Write incorrect responses above the test letter or word for future error analysis.

PART I

Number Correct

Naming Upper Case Letters

X	G	O	K	B	I	D	M	T	U	F	W	A
C	H	J	R	N	E	Z	S	Q	L	P	Y	V

/26

Naming Lower Case Letters

o	w	r	a	b	k	e	m	d	y	t	u	x
f	c	i	v	g	h	j	n	q	s	z	l	p

/26

Giving Letter Sounds

s	t	n	p	f	d	c	u	l	o	y	r	k
x	i	b	j	a	m	h	v	e	z	g	w	q

/26

Giving Consonant Digraph Sounds

ch   sh   wh   th (this)   th (thimble)   ck

/6

Directions: Have the pupil read by column

PHONETIC WORDS

Mixed

ban	dug	bud	hum	ten
fed	pin	met	not	lug
did	nod	ham	box	rib
lag	men	fix	peg	sup
cog	pig	pep	fun	jap

/25

Patterned

an	it	dog	gum	bed
ban	bit	fog	hum	fed
can	fit	hog	mum	led
Dan	hit	jog	rum	Ned
fan	kit	log	sum	red

/25

Decoding Skills Test—p. 2 (Examiner's Copy)

PART II

READING: PHONETIC WORDS: REGULAR PATTERNS

Directions: Present *Real Words* student copy reading list to child. Say, "These are real words. Start here (point) and read across." Write mispronounced element above word (for future error analysis). Word is counted as incorrect when underlined element is mispronounced.

Mastery: Circle correct responses.

Number Correct

Consonant & Short Vowel

| gas | pit | nip | yam | Rex | /10 |
| fig | mop | den | kit | jab | |

2-Letter Consonant Blends & Digraphs

| scat | grand | dwelt | snag | smash | /10 |
| chin | shed | Phil | path | rich | |

Long Vowels

| tide | rule | mail | team | yoke | /10 |
| take | seek | pie | loan | more | |

3-Letter Consonant Blends

| shrub | split | sprint | squid | thrash | /10 |
| scrap | throw | squish | strong | splash | |

'r' Controlled Vowels

| corn | fern | church | shirt | star | /10 |
| earn | turn | mirth | park | berth | |

Vowel Variants

| cause | straw | threw | brook | food | /10 |
| toy | foil | loud | stew | paw | |

Basic Sight Words Test—Level I

Student's Name _____
Age _____
Examiner _____
Fall Date _____
Spring Date _____

Basic Sight Words Test—Level I
(Examiner's Copy)

Directions: Show flashcards to the student. Have the student read the words on the flashcards.

Mastery: Record a plus (+) in the space provided if the student responds correctly without teacher assistance. Write in incorrect responses for later analysis. Write in "D.K." if the student responds "don't know."

	1st check	flash-card	2nd check		1st check	flash-card	2nd check
a				me			
I				look			
too				can			
the				good			
in				brown			
to				six			
see				be			
into				today			
and				not			
two				little			

Basic Sight Words Test—Level I, p. 2

	1st check	flash-card	2nd check		1st check	flash-card	2nd check
up				one			
blue				black			
she				my			
yellow				at			
he				all			
go				so			
you				by			
we				do			
big				are			
red				him			
jump				her			
it				on			
play				green			
down				eat			
for				four			
old				said			
is				away			
run							

San Diego Quick Assessment Test

Student's Name _____
Age _____
Examiner _____
Fall Date _____
Spring Date _____

San Diego Quick Assessment Test
(Examiner's Copy)

Directions: Beginning with the preprimer list of words, have student read from increasingly difficult lists on 3" x 5" cards until three words are missed.

Mastery: Circle correct responses. Write incorrect responses in space below under Error Analysis. Record reading levels: Independent (1 error) _____
Instructional (2 errors) _____
Frustration (3 errors) _____

Error Analysis:

Preprimer	Primer	First Grade	Second Grade
see	you	road	our
play	come	live	please
me	not	thank	myself
at	with	when	town
run	jump	bigger	early
go	help	how	send .
and	is	always	wide
look	work	night	believe
can	are	spring	quietly
here	this	today	carefully

San Diego Quick Assessment Test—p. 2

Third Grade	Fourth Grade	Fifth Grade	Sixth Grade
city	decided	scanty	bridge
middle	served	certainly	commercial
moment	amazed	develop	abolish
frightened	silent	considered	trucker
exclaimed	wrecked	discussed	apparatus
several	improved	behaved	elementary
lonely	certainly	splendid	comment
drew	entered	acquainted	necessity
since	realized	escaped	gallery
straight	interrupted	grim	relativity

Seventh Grade	Eighth Grade	Ninth Grade	Tenth Grade
amber	capacious	conscientious	zany
dominion	limitation	isolation	jerkin
sundry	pretext	molecule	nausea
capillary	intrigue	ritual	gratuitous
impetuous	delusion	momentous	linear
blight	immaculate	vulnerable	inept
wrest	ascent	kinship	legality
enumerate	acrid	conservatism	aspen
daunted	binocular	jaunty	amnesty
condescend	embankment	inventive	barometer

Temporal Concepts Test

Student's Name _____
Age _____
Examiner _____
Fall Date _____
Spring Date _____

Temporal Concepts Test
(Examiner's Copy)

Directions: Ask student each question. Repeat the question if necessary but indicate that repetition was needed. Record *exact* response.

Comments:

I. CONCEPT

A. Past
1. What day was yesterday? _____
2. What did you do last night? _____
3. Did you go to school yesterday? _____
4. What did you eat for breakfast today? _____
5. What did you do before breakfast? _____
6. What did you do last summer? _____
7. What grade were you in last year? _____

B. Present
1. What day is today? _____
2. How old are you now? _____
3. What are you doing now? _____
4. Where is your father today? _____
5. Are you eating lunch at home today? _____
6. Where is your mother? _____

C. Future
1. What day will tomorrow be? _____
2. How old will you be on your next birthday? _____
3. Where will you sleep tonight? _____
4. Where will you be tomorrow? _____
5. When are you going home? _____
6. What grade will you be in next year? _____
7. What are you doing after school today? _____

Temporal Concepts Test—p. 2

D. Relationships—Before and After

1. What day comes after Sunday? _____
2. What do you do after dinner? _____
3. What day comes before Friday? _____
4. What month comes before March? _____
5. What month comes after June? _____
6. What month comes before January? _____
7. What year comes after this one? _____
8. What meal comes before lunch? _____ .
9. What season comes before summer? _____
10. When does the sun come up (get light)? _____

E. Relationships—Length of Time

1. Which is longer, a day or a week? _____
2. Which is longer, a month or a year? _____
3. Is an hour shorter than a minute? _____
4. Is a year shorter than a month? _____
5. Which is shorter, a second or a minute? _____
6. Which is shorter, an hour or a half hour? _____

II. AUTOMATIC

A. Sunday—Monday—Tuesday—Wednesday—Thursday—
Friday—Saturday   No. _____

B. January—February—March—April—May—June—July—
August—September—October—November—December
No. _____

C. Spring—Summer—Fall (Autumn)—Winter   No. _____

D. How many?

Seconds in a minute? ____   Days in a month? _____

Minutes in an hour? _____   Days in a year?   _____

Hours in a day?   _____   Weeks in a year? _____

III. CLOCK

A. Set: 1. 6:00 _____   **B. Read:** 1. 5:00 _____

2. 3:30 _____   2. 12:30 _____

3. 1:15 _____   3. 3:15 _____

4. 5:45 _____   4. 4:45 _____

5. 7:25 _____   5. 9:55 _____

Reading Numbers Test

Student's Name _____
Age _____
Examiner _____
Fall Date _____
Spring Date _____

Reading Numbers Test
(Examiner's Copy)

Directions: Ask the student to read aloud the numbers in row 1. Give these oral directions: "When I say begin, read each of the numbers as well as you can. Ready . . . begin."

Scoring: Cross out each number skipped or identified incorrectly. Write in incorrect responses. Circle the *last* number identified.

		Highest Number Identified
ROW 1	0 7 5 2 4 9 8 1 3 6	1–10 __
ROW 2	13 19 16 11 15 18 12 17 10 14	11–20 __
ROW 3	21 30 39 25 34 27 33 24 36 29	21–40 __
ROW 4	76 96 52 47 82 43 74 69 54 98	40–100 __

Comments:

Math Assessment Test Record Sheet

Student's Name _____
Age _____
Examiner _____
Fall Date _____
Spring Date _____

Math Assessment Test Record Sheet	Total Possible	Fall Total	Spring Total
ADDITION			
Basic Facts—sums to 10	5		
Basic Facts—sums to 18	5		
2 digit, 2 addends, no regrouping	3		
3 digit, 2 addends, no regrouping	3		
Carrying from 1 place	3		
Carrying from 10 place	3		
3 or more addends	3		
3 or more digits, consecutive regrouping	3		
SUBTRACTION			
Basic Facts—minuends less than 10	5		
Basic Facts—minuends less than 20	5		
2 digit, no regrouping	3		
3 digit, no regrouping	3		
Regrouping from 10s column	3		
Regrouping from 100s column	3		
Subtraction with 0s in minuend	3		
3 or more digits, consecutive regrouping	3		
MULTIPLICATION			
Basic Facts	8		
1 2-digit factor, no regrouping	3		
2 2-digit factors, no regrouping	3		
1 2-digit factor, regrouping	3		
2 or more digit factors, regrouping	3		
Multiple multiplication—no regrouping	2		
Multiple multiplication—regrouping	2		
DIVISION			
Basic Facts	4		
1 place divisor—even	3		
1 place divisor—uneven, no remainder	3		
1 place divisor—uneven, remainder	3		
2 place divisors—easy types	3		
2 place divisors—complex types	2		
2 place divisors—estimation	2		
2 place divisors—zeros in quotients	2		

Observations:

Physical Skills Test Explanation Sheet

Physical Skills Test Explanation Sheet

Directions: Have the child demonstrate the following gross-motor and lateralization skills. Record observations and ratings on the record sheet. In each case, note whether the activity is adequate or inadequate. (See record sheet for detailed recording instructions.)

I. Gross-Motor Skills: Have the child perform each of the following movements.

- Standing   Have child stand in normal position. Note position of head—either held too far forward, backward, or to one side; shoulders unusually rounded or tilted; a curvature of the spine ("sway back"); habitual standing on one leg; a tilting hip position; or any unusual position of the knees and feet.

- Sitting   Have child sit in normal position. Note habitual hip and back position and position of head.

- Balance   Have child walk a chalk line on the floor. Note degree of difficulty in maintaining upright position.

- Walking   Have child walk across room or playground. Note any unusual quality in gait.

- Running   Have child run a short distance. Note any unusual stride or awkwardness.

- Jumping   Have child jump three or four times. Note degree of difficulty in moving body and maintaining balance.

- Skipping   Have child skip a short distance. Note degree of difficulty in moving body and maintaining balance.

- Hopping   Have child hop a short distance. Note degree of difficulty in moving body and maintaining balance.

Physical Skills Test Explanation Sheet—p. 2

II. Lateralization Skills: Have the child perform each of the following activities *four* times.

- Pencil Pick-up   Place the pencil on the table and ask the child to pick it up and write or draw. Note hand used and transfer.

- Paper Pick-up   Say: "Are you good at pretending? I'm going to throw this ball (as you crumple a piece of paper into ball shape) so that it lands at your feet. See if you can pick it up and throw it back to me." Note both pick-up preference and throw preference in this activity.

- Pointing   Say: "Point to the door. Now, put your hand down. This time, point to the chair. Put your hand down again. Point to me. Put your hand down. Now, point to the desk." Record each response.

- Throwing   Check at the same time as pick-up.

- Kicking   Say: (using the same crumpled paper) "Now pretend this is a bigger ball. It is a kick ball this time. I will roll it and you kick it." (Roll the ball, aiming alternately to the right foot and then the left foot.) Note what the child does to get the ball in position.

- Hopping   Designate a starting position and say: "Hop on one foot all the way over to me and touch my hand." Note which foot is chosen.

- Telescope Viewing   Roll a piece of paper into a tube and say: "Can you pretend this is a telescope? Put it up to your eye and look at the door knob. Now, put it down. Now put it up to your eye and look at my pencil. Put it down again. This time look at this spot on the chair." Continue naming objects for the child to view. Indicate the eye the child preferred. Also indicate which hand was used.

Physical Skills Test Record Sheet

Student's Name _____
Age _____
Examiner _____
Fall Date _____
Spring Date _____

Physical Skills Test Record Sheet

Physical Skills Test Record Sheet

I. **Gross Motor Skills:** Describe any unusual problem, inadequacy, or clumsiness. Rate as adequate or inadequate.

   a. Standing—

   b. Sitting—

   c. Balance—

   d. Walking—

   e. Running—

   f. Jumping—

   g. Skipping—

   h. Hopping—

II. **Lateralization Skills:** Record hand, foot, and eye preference. Record with "R" or "L" to indicate preference.

Hand:	Pencil	1 ___	2 ___	3 ___	4 ___
	Pick-up	1 ___	2 ___	3 ___	4 ___
	Pointing	1 ___	2 ___	3 ___	4 ___
	Throwing (a ball)	1 ___	2 ___	3 ___	4 ___
Foot:	Kicking (a ball)	1 ___	2 ___	3 ___	4 ___
	Hopping	1 ___	2 ___	3 ___	4 ___
Eye:	Telescope (use rolled up paper)	1H___	2H___	3H___	4H___
		1E___	2E___	3E___	4E___

Academic Record Sheet

Reading and Language Record
on <u>Sally Jones</u>

Year <u>1977–78</u>
Teacher <u>S. Gappa</u>
E.H. Special Class

Book/Skill	Date Started	Date Completed	Comments
Sound-symbol relationship for m, o, d, c, a, g, h, j, a, k, p, i, r, t, u, f	9/77		11/77—Does not use independently. Provide extra practice.
Dolch words— Level I	9/77	1/78	1/78—Able to read 53/55. Review *of* and *away.*
Last half of "Around the Corner" and workbook (began last year)	9/77	11/77	11/77—Could not do rhyming words on achievement test, but adequate scores on word recognition and comprehension. Ready for next level.

An individual record sheet is used to record the child's progress in each academic area.

Color Word Recognition Test

Student's Name _____
Age _____
Examiner _____
Fall Date _____
Spring Date _____

Color Word Recognition Test
(Examiner's Copy)

Directions: Show the child the colored blocks or colored objects. Point to each and have the child name the color.

Mastery: Record a plus (+) for a correct response. Write in an incorrect response.

I. Can name colors when shown colored blocks or objects.

	FALL	SPRING		FALL	SPRING
white			red		
brown			black		
yellow			orange		
purple			blue		
			green		

II. Can match color words to colored blocks or objects.

	FALL	SPRING		FALL	SPRING
white			red		
brown			black		
yellow			orange		
purple			blue		
			green		

Books We've Found Most Useful

Glasser, William. *Schools Without Failure.* New York: Harper and Row, 1969.

Discusses the use of a class meeting as a means to help children express feelings and concerns, and to develop problem-solving skills. This book is a good model for a teacher to use in setting up and implementing such meetings.

Gordon, Thomas. *Parent Effectiveness Training.* New York: Peter H. Wyden, 1971.

Presents a "no lose" program for helping parents work effectively with their children, with strong emphasis on clear and specific communications. Advocates the child participating actively in seeking solutions. Basis for many of the parent effectiveness classes now offered.

Kaluger, George, and Kolson, Clifford J. *Reading and Learning Disabilities.* Columbus, Ohio: Charles E. Merrill, 1969.

Good on formal and informal diagnostic tools, with specific recommendations for remediation. Excellent bibliographies at the end of each chapter.

Kroth, Roger L. *Communicating with Parents of Exceptional Children.* Denver, Colorado: Love Publishing, 1975.

Very practical suggestions on the when, why, and how of various ways of communicating with parents and getting their support for the in-school program and at home. Provides appendix of selected readings for parents of all types of exceptional children.

Slingerland, Beth. *A Multi-Sensory Approach to Language Arts for Specific Language Disability Children.* Cambridge, Massachusetts: Educator's Publishing Service, 1976.

Step-by-step procedures for teaching reading, writing, and spelling skills using a multi-sensory approach. Basis for the teacher education classes on the "Slingerland" method offered every summer in various cities in the United States.

Tarnopol, Lester, ed. *Learning Disabilities—Introduction to Educational and Medical Management.* Springfield, Illinois: Charles C. Thomas, 1969.

Includes both medical and psychiatric perspectives and management ideas by leading authorities. Useful appendix listing organizations of parents for children with learning disabilities.

Traub, Nina, with Frances Bloom et al. *Recipe for Reading: A Structured Approach to Linguistics.* Cambridge, Massachusetts: Educator's Publishing Service, 1975.

Begins with strategies for the sequential presentation of specific letter sounds, and then progresses to teaching more complex aspects of language. "At the fingertips" lists of phonetic words, phrases and sentences.

01436 7750